C000227258

# ANTI-TOTALITARIANISM:
# THE LEFT-WING CASE
# FOR A NEOCONSERVATIVE
# FOREIGN POLICY

# ANTI-TOTALITARIANISM: THE LEFT-WING CASE FOR A NEOCONSERVATIVE FOREIGN POLICY

Oliver Kamm

© The Social Affairs Unit 2005

British Library Cataloguing in Publication Data
A catalogue record of this book is available from the British Library

All views expressed in this publication are those of the author, not those
of the Social Affairs Unit, its Trustees, Advisers or Director

Cover photograph:
© Network Photographers/Alamy

Book production by Crowley Esmonde Limited
Printed and bound in the United Kingdom


ISBN 1-904863-06-X

Social Affairs Unit
314-322 Regent Street
London W1B 5SA
www.socialaffairsunit.org.uk

For Louise, Eleanor and Alexandra

# CONTENTS

Foreword by Martin Bell, OBE                                     11

Introduction                                                     15

CHAPTER 1  Liberalism, the Left and Collective Security:         25
           pre-war precursors

CHAPTER 2  The Left and the Cold Wars                            43

CHAPTER 3  Regime Change                                         67

CHAPTER 4  The Task for the Left                                 97

The Author                                                      127

# ACKNOWLEDGEMENTS

I am grateful to Michael Mosbacher for suggesting I write this book; to the Social Affairs Unit for publishing it; to Martin Bell for his foreword; and to Daniel Finkelstein of *The Times* for allowing me space in the newspaper to argue for many of the views presented here.

It has long been my ambition to express in print my intellectual debt to the writings of the late pragmatist philosopher, socialist, scholar of Marxism and foe of totalitarianism Sidney Hook, who is quoted at the start of Chapter 4.

# FOREWORD

*Anti-totalitarianism: The Left-Wing Case for a Neoconservative Foreign Policy* is not just a book but a literary siege gun. Its audacious thesis, that 'the neoconservative stance accords with the historic values of the democratic Left', arises not only from a justification of the invasion of Iraq in March 2003, but from a broader analysis of past debates about national security, on both sides of the Atlantic. It tests and challenges the orthodox view, held by almost everyone I meet (except Oliver Kamm), that the Iraq war was a monumental error by the British and Americans, and that the United Kingdom's participation in it was the worst mistake made by a British Prime Minister in my lifetime. The author is no mean warrior himself. His words are his cannonballs. And he trains them on our certainty that we were right in opposing a war fought on a whim about regime change and a falsehood about weapons of mass destruction.

It takes an original thinker to propose, conversely, that 'Iraq was not the biggest blunder since Suez: it was the most far-sighted and noble act of British foreign policy since the founding of Nato.' ('That will take some arguing', he bravely admits.) Oliver Kamm is indeed an original thinker. He also happens to be my nephew, so I have known him for longer than most. And I have profited from the connection: he was my issues adviser and all-purpose behind-the-scenes guru in the campaign to unseat Neil Hamilton in Tatton in 1997. Oliver is, in general, incapable of writing a dull sentence. The only exception was my election manifesto, which he drafted deliberately to make it as boring as possible. The sections on the economy were so anaesthetically contrived that my opponents were (I believe) unable to read them without falling asleep, and therefore to pick them apart. This modest strategy helped to deliver the required result.

Oliver has always been political, but having had the benefit of his views for some 30 years, I do not believe his thinking has developed in an altogether straight line of march. He started on the progressive Left and believes that he still belongs there. Readers can judge the validity of that claim for themselves. Perhaps he is more of the radical centre, if such a place exists. I believe that the Tatton experience politicised him still further, to the point that he understood the difference that an individual can make by words as well as deeds. He grew tired of being an onlooker, and wished to play a part in shaping the debate. This he has been doing most effectively in his web log, which is widely read and respected at home and abroad – even, and perhaps especially, by those who disagree with him. His regular columns in *The Times* have also brought him to the attention of a wider audience. Sometimes I detect the influence of G. K. Chesterton, whom we both admire. He is always at his best when defending the indefensible – that is, indefensible to me, but never to him. The case that he makes does indeed take some arguing; but he argues it with style, dexterity and scholarship.

An opinion never exposed to challenge is not an opinion worth holding, but merely a prejudice. An opinion exposed to Oliver Kamm's siege-gun tactics will be challenged to the limit in the heat of the battle of ideas. In my own case, on the central issue of the war in Iraq, some of the outer fortifications crumbled, yet the central citadel held. But that was at first contact and under the opening barrage. On a second reading, of this one-of-a-kind book by a one-of-a-kind writer, the damage may be greater and more structural.

MARTIN BELL

# INTRODUCTION

## THE LEFT AND NATIONAL SECURITY

Throughout its history – at least since the Second International fractured over the support given by social democrats to their respective national sides in World War I – the Left has been split on the issue of national security. This book recounts historical debates on the British Left over four such episodes: collective security to counter fascist aggression in the 1930s; the Attlee Government's hostility to the Soviet Union after World War II; the Labour Party's rejection in the 1980s of that anti-Communist inheritance; and regime change in Afghanistan and Iraq after the terrorist atrocities of 11 September 2001.

The common thread of these episodes is Britain's response, in concert with its allies, to totalitarianism. I believe there are instructive points of comparison between earlier debates and current controversies. Fitting politics to an antecedent scheme is a Procrustean heresy identified by the philosopher Michael Oakeshott as 'Rationalism',[1] but in the case of the Baathist regime lately overthrown in Iraq there are genuine parallels with earlier variants of totalitarianism. Baathism was an ideology developed in the 1930s under the influence of European fascism, and Saddam Hussein consciously modelled his rule on those of Hitler and Stalin. In fashioning a foreign policy for the early 21st century, progressives need an awareness of history.

The premise of this book is that a Left uninterested in defending the constitutional societies of the West, in its broadest sense, cannot serve progressive ends. The issue ought to be particularly clear when the principal adversary of the Western democracies is a form of totalitarianism both with recognisable twentieth-century forebears and with a still more atavistic – literally mediaeval – character.

Extraordinarily, for some parts of the Left it is not. It took almost no time at all after terrorists destroyed the Twin Towers for their hatred to be rationalised, or at least relativised, by longstanding critics of US power. Noam Chomsky declared: 'We can think of the United States as an "innocent victim" only if we adopt the convenient path of ignoring the record of its actions and those of its allies, which are, after all, hardly a secret.'[2] Even if the entire charge sheet constructed by Chomsky over several decades were correct in every detail, the civilians killed in New York, Pennsylvania and Washington on 9/11 – of whom there might have been thousands more – would still, indeed, be innocent victims. Moreover, the record of US actions – again, accepting for the sake of argument that Chomsky renders it accurately – is redundant as an explanation of Islamist terrorism.

It is a failing of many liberal commentators to be swayed by the sheer unlikelihood of a popular movement dedicated to the political realisation of an eschatological vision. So far as we can ascertain from their intended targets, and in the absence of a suicide note, the terrorists of 9/11 were not making a statement about poverty or oppression. Rather, they were acting out an ideological imperative of striking at the institutions of Western civilisation: constitutional government, international commerce and a civilian-controlled military. Whereas in UK debate the arguments about regime change have centred on tendentious assessments of the role of neoconservative intellectuals in the Bush Administration, there is a less Machiavellian explanation for the US-led and UK-supported strategy of toppling dictators. That is the link – a genuine 'root cause' of terrorism – between autocracy and theocratic fanaticism.

The men who flew aeroplanes into office blocks, killing 3,000 civilians of some 80 nationalities, opposed the US and its allies not for any sins of commission or omission on our part, but for what we are: liberal, secular, pluralist and tolerant. We cannot pacify al-Qaeda without surrendering our values, and even that would be insufficient. A movement driven by violent millenarianism may engage in political tactics, but does not have negotiable ends – which, given the extreme undesirability of conforming to their demands, is just as well. All that is open to us is to counter the present danger through persuasive diplomacy (not with our declared enemies, but with our actual and potential allies), vastly improved intelligence, and, ultimately, force and the continuing threat of it.

Earlier historical debates on the Left contain much that is salutary as well as suggestive. The temptation to temporise the ideological character of the declared enemies of Western civilisation is a recurring one. At best, this is a genuflection to a 'realism' that, in the belief that peace is maintained by a balance of power, understates the ideological dimensions of the anti-totalitarian struggle. But in other cases it represents a long-standing belief on some parts of the Left that the enemy is at home – the imperfect but civilised democracies of the liberal West. The dividing line between this stance – really a gut prejudice, if not an affectation – and outright support for totalitarianism is thin. The historical idiosyncrasy of the debates since 9/11 is not that some parts of the Left excuse or identify with totalitarianism, but that an alliance has emerged between different and previously hostile forms of totalitarianism.

## REGIME CHANGE AND DOMESTIC POLITICS

Though foreign policy featured prominently in the 2005 general election campaign, the issue of totalitarianism did not. Having allied with the US administration in the Iraq War, Tony Blair resolved that the issue could only lose him votes, and that he should therefore try to shift political debate on to domestic issues. His endeavours were largely unsuccessful. He returned to office a weakened figure and with a sharply reduced majority.

Not the least of Blair's problems was the ineptitude with which the case for war had initially been prosecuted. The Bush Administration's speculative hypothesis of direct links between Saddam Hussein and al-Qaeda remained unproved. The widespread perception that Bush and Blair had been dishonest in urging war to pre-empt Saddam's military capabilities was buttressed by the failure to find stockpiles of biological and chemical weapons in liberated Iraq.

The case for regime change was stronger than that. It merited support, especially from those subscribing to liberal and progressive values. Its urgency was emphasised only three months after the election with the first suicide bombings to take place in London, killing more than 50 people. The Prime Minister was widely praised then for his resolution and composure in the face of terrorism; the cogency of his case for regime change as an integral part of anti-terrorist strategy ought also to be acknowledged. This book is intended to advance that argument by placing it in historical perspective.

By way of explanation of my own position: I am a left-winger and Labour sympathiser of almost 30 years' standing. I first canvassed for Labour in the 1979 general election. I even supported the party in 1983 under Michael Foot. I played a minor role in the 1980s as Chairman of the Oxford University Labour Club, a Labour activist in Lambeth, and a constituency member of the moderate Labour Solidarity Campaign, in trying to return Labour to its traditional Atlanticism. While I allowed my party membership to lapse in the late 1980s and have never felt sufficiently strongly to renew it, I welcomed the apparent determination of Tony Blair, on being elected leader in 1994, to jettison what remained of Labour's ideological commitments from the 1980s and fashion a more coherent social democracy.

Much of Blair's promise has been unfulfilled, reflecting an unwillingness to recognise that, in the celebrated but still important maxim of Pierre Mendes-France, '*Gouverner, c'est choisir*'. It is not even that Blairism lacks a language of priorities: more fundamental, it fails to recognise that not all things we value are compatible. But on foreign policy, Blair represents something distinctive. This is insufficiently understood even by his critics. Orthodoxy within and outside the Labour Party holds that Iraq was an unnecessary war founded on Blair's perplexing lack of judgement, which caused his electoral rebuff. In the view of former Foreign Secretary Robin Cook, 'it seems only too likely that the judgement of history may be that the invasion of Iraq has been the biggest blunder in British foreign and security policy in the half century since

Suez'.[3] The widespread belief that Blair was, at the least, indifferent to the demands of truth in his presentation of the case for war underlines, in this view, the contingent and aberrant character of the issue.

My view is different. Blair's position has been more consistent than his critics suppose. In many respects it has been admirable. Long before 9/11, Blair abandoned the conservative 'realism' – more accurately, amoral quietism – that had characterised John Major's foreign policies. Rather than acquiescing in Serb aggression, Blair confronted it. Out of humanitarian obligation and an awareness that failed states breed fanaticism, he sent British troops to preserve Sierra Leone from hand-lopping rebels. Iraq was not the biggest blunder since Suez: it was the most far-sighted and noble act of British foreign policy since the founding of Nato. Blair's record exemplifies foreign policy 'with an ethical dimension'.

Before the election, *bien-pensant* academics asserted that a vote for Blair was a vote for Bush.[4] The reverse was true: President Bush, who as a candidate in the presidential election of 2000 had denounced interventionist 'nation-building', adopted Blairism. After 9/11, Bush's instinctive conservatism gave way to promoting global democracy as our defence against theocratic barbarism – a strategy that accords with traditional liberal-democratic internationalism.

As a result, and to my pleasurable astonishment, in the 2005 election the party of Michael Foot was the sole representative of a credible defence policy. The Tories' tergiversations over Iraq were too cynical even to be dignified with the term 'opportunism'; the Liberal Democrats' predictions about the war (the inevitable refugee crisis; the stymieing of Israeli–Palestinian peace talks) were consistently wrong.

This was a brave stance for Blair to adopt. There is no question but that he damaged his political standing by committing troops to the Iraq War; had the war not taken place, we can reasonably assume that he would have enjoyed a substantial and – given its unprecedented character in Labour politics – triumphant third election victory. Many, probably almost all, Labour supporters would regard this as an indictment of the PM. I regard it as a measure of the man's political stature. Knowing that the character of the international order had changed since the Cold War and not just since 9/11, Blair chose to ally himself with a nominally conservative US administration in a war that needed to be fought, when the policy of containment of Saddam Hussein had failed, and the toleration of autocratic states in the region was both an affront to our values and an emerging – though not an imminent – threat to our security. The threat consisted in the confluence of failed states, the likely proliferation of nuclear technologies, and terrorist groups driven by religious fanaticism more than specific grievances.

The polarising effect of Iraq has encouraged a highly personalised Opposition campaign against the Prime Minister on grounds of his alleged lack of integrity, and a culture of dissent among Labour MPs who make a virtue of having opposed the war. This book argues for the consistency of an interventionist foreign policy with the humanitarian and progressive traditions of the Left, and urges a coalition in British politics to replicate the one that, with varying degrees of resolve, supported liberal-democratic internationalist opposition to totalitarianism before and after World War II. It is also an appeal to my fellow-leftists to acknowledge that the Bush–Blair strategy in foreign affairs accords with our movement's ideals. We should support the current trajectory of US strategic doctrine – not because it gives us leverage over a conservative US administration, but because it is a natural cause for those with a visceral opposition to fascism and clerical reaction.

That will take some arguing. My own apprehension about the state of opinion in the Labour Party caused me to switch my vote in 2005. I had the choice of a Labour candidate who declared in advance her intention of opposing the foreign policies of the Government, or a Conservative candidate who, I was confident, would support them (and who also held more liberal views on social issues than were expressed in the lamentable and unpleasant national Conservative campaign). Both these candidates were pursuing heterodox positions. A consistent conservative will be wary of the unanticipated consequences of regime change, while confronting tyranny and promoting global democracy are causes that the Left should instinctively support. Both liberals and conservatives ought to be able to agree on the prudential grounds for an interventionist foreign policy, however – and the creation of such a coalition is the most important, the overriding, political issue of our times.

On those grounds, as a committed left-winger and in order to support Tony Blair, I cast my first ever Conservative vote. To the extent that anyone locally will have noticed my argument, which was published in *The Times* shortly before polling day, it will not have helped the candidate I endorsed, who lost by a few hundred votes.

## SUMMARY OF THE ARGUMENT

Chapters 1 and 2 discuss earlier episodes of splits on the Left over how best to deal with totalitarianism. These are, first, the varying responses in the UK to the emerging totalitarian threat of fascism in the 1930s, and secondly the debates surrounding the Attlee Government's support for the Truman Doctrine. Having taken a long time to shed its illusions about both non-violence and the pacific character of collective security in the 1930s, the non-Communist Left supported democracy overseas and in many respects played an essential role in its defence in the immediate post-war years. It did so against a small but persistent opposition from those who favoured a non-aligned foreign policy, as well as from a durable pro-Communist element in the labour and trade union movement. In 1945 Labour understood that the liberal democracies faced a totalitarian threat that would exist regardless of what foreign or domestic policies a left-wing government adopted. That was the nature of Soviet Communism, and Labour made a right and necessary decision to ally itself with the United States. It also expelled from membership a parliamentary caucus that not only disagreed with that approach but also explicitly defended Soviet expansionism and repression.

Chapter 2 further discusses the dilution of that tradition of liberal-democratic and socialist internationalism in the 1970s, and especially the 1980s, in anti-nuclear campaigns directed most particularly against the Administration of Ronald Reagan. This was more than a little ironic, given that President Reagan, unlike all other Presidents since 1945, and to the horror of his European allies, shared the campaigners' vision of a nuclear-free world.

Chapter 3 discusses the response of the Left since 9/11 to Islamist terrorism and the wars to overthrow repressive regimes in Afghanistan and Iraq. Invoking recent research that suggests the 'root cause' of terrorism is not poverty but autocracy, it argues that Western security requires the promotion of democracy. This is the proper justification for regime change, as distinct from the case the Bush Administration actually made. There was scant evidence of direct links between Saddam Hussein and al-Qaeda, or of Iraq's being implicated in 9/11. But Saddam welcomed the destruction of the Twin Towers when even repressive governments previously accommodating to the Taliban (i.e. Saudi Arabia and Pakistan) were becoming more cautious in their public pronouncements. He did not possess weapons of mass destruction (WMD) in any usable form, but he sought that capability by stealth in defiance of the UN Security Council Resolutions that had marked the terms of ceasefire in the first Gulf War. He was not an imminent threat, but he was an inevitable one, and a progressive Left ought to have welcomed a military campaign (there being no other course available) to overthrow him.

Chapter 4 sets out the principles of a progressive foreign policy. The first is militant opposition to theocratic reaction, in the same way and for the same reason that anti-fascism and liberal anti-Communism were axioms of an earlier Left. The British Left should acknowledge President Bush's discontinuity from earlier flawed approaches in foreign policy. As well as marking a welcome turn from a willingness to ally with authoritarian regimes during the Cold War, current US policy is also (contrary to the implicit assumptions of many of its right-wing advocates) more radical than the stance of the conservatives' hero, Ronald Reagan. Reagan was instinctively wary of using direct military force, prudently managed the superpower relationship when he realised that Communism was a spent force (an option not open to today's leaders confronting Islamist totalitarianism), implicitly accepted the notion of an imposed Middle East peace settlement without pressing for democratic change in the Palestinian national movement, and withdrew US forces from Lebanon after the 1983 terrorist murder of 242 marines.

Surveying the historical background, the chapter concludes that Tony Blair's foreign policy – and particularly his statement of that case in his address to the US Congress in July 2003 – is a reassertion of an earlier left-wing tradition. But unlike some left-wing sympathisers of Tony Blair, I accept, with caveats, the term neoconservative as applied to his foreign policy. Indeed, the neoconservative stance accords with the historic values of the democratic Left, and neoconservatism itself should be seen as a contemporary variant of traditional liberal internationalism (though one with less stress on the role of international institutions).

Interventionism has been a difficult case to argue in British politics. In the recent general election campaign Tony Blair scarcely tried, for fear of provoking still more defections among Labour voters. That cause must, nonetheless, be taken up, particularly by the Left, for we cannot be true to our traditions and values without it. As in the Cold War, the Left has a historically important task in witnessing to those ideals and representing them in a wider anti-totalitarian coalition.

1 Michael Oakeshott, 'Rationalism in politics', in *Rationalism in Politics and Other Essays*, ed. T. Fuller (Indianapolis: Liberty Fund, 1991).

2 Noam Chomsky, *9/11* (New York: Seven Stories Press, 2001), p. 35.

3 Robin Cook, 'The invasion of Iraq was Britain's worst foreign policy blunder since Suez', *Independent*, 19 March 2004.

4 For example Richard Dawkins, 'Why I'm backing the heroic stand of Reg Keys', *Independent*, 23 April 2005. Keys, the father of a British serviceman murdered in Iraq, stood as an independent anti-war candidate in Tony Blair's constituency in the general election. He was probably not assisted by grandiloquent claims from his celebrity supporters about his prospects for victory, but gained a respectable 10% of the vote nonetheless.

# CHAPTER 1

## LIBERALISM, THE LEFT AND COLLECTIVE SECURITY: PRE-WAR PRECURSORS

*It will be necessary for the western democracies, even at some extension of their risks, to gather round them all the elements of collective security or, if you prefer to call it so, combined defensive strength against aggression – the phrase which I prefer – which can be assembled on the basis of the Covenant of the League of Nations.*
Winston Churchill, November 1936

### AMBIGUITIES OF COLLECTIVE SECURITY

Churchill's language in attacking the policies of a government from which he had been excluded was carefully chosen. The notion of collective security through the League of Nations had gained support in British politics (it commanded near-universal assent on the Centre and Left) in the early 1930s owing to its promise of a peaceful way of resolving disputes and avoiding the destructiveness of another world war. As the decade progressed, however, collective security became a more ambiguous concept. The logic of collective action in the furtherance of peace implied an assertion of countervailing military strength by the democracies operating under the Covenant of the League. In practice, the expansionism of the Axis powers received a less resolute response.

There were two main problems, one organisational and one philosophical. The first was that the League was deprived of American support by the exigencies of domestic politics. This was not merely a nativist distrust of international entanglements: there were serious questions about proposed US participation in the League in the aftermath of World War I, and these remained unanswered by the American President

Woodrow Wilson. Article X of the League of Nations Charter committed member states to 'preserve as against external aggression the territorial integrity and existing political independence of all members of the League'.

The plain meaning of this phrase was that the US and other member states were obliged to take up arms, against an aggressor, at the behest of the League's Council. This was difficult to square with the US Constitutional provision that Congress reserved to itself the right to declare war. If the League's member states were not so obliged, then the League was not a sovereign enforcer against international lawlessness. As one of the League's Congressional critics, Senator William Borah of Idaho, demanded of Wilson: 'What will your league amount to if it does not contain powers that no one dreams of giving it?'[1] Wilson gave an evasive answer to the effect that the League's provisions would be morally, if not legally, binding, and that moral suasion would be sufficient. The absurdity of this claim was not lost on the creators of the League's successor, the United Nations Organisation, after World War II, and to this day illuminates the quandary of those who wish to subject *raisons d'état* to the rule of international law.

The second problem, much evident in British political debate though not limited to it, was that to some of its exponents, collective security continued to mean diplomatic pursuit of conciliation. This led them to align with the very tradition they wished to supersede, namely the upholding of balance of power as a means of avoiding war. No one better exemplified this aim than Sir Herbert Samuel, Liberal leader from 1931 to 1935 and Home Secretary in the National Government, who was so convinced of the merits of the Munich agreement that Neville Chamberlain offered him a Cabinet post. The former Labour leader George Lansbury and the anti-militarist Independent Labour Party also passionately supported diplomatic openings to Hitler. Churchill, with the support of the non-pacifist successor leaders of Labour and the Liberals, aimed to stiffen the notion of collective security.

## THE LEGACY OF WORLD WAR I

British policymaking in the 1930s was overshadowed by memories of the destructiveness of the First World War. This had led to a strong belief among liberals in the virtues of collective security through international organisation, as declaimed by President Wilson in his declaration of war on Germany in 1917 (and many times thereafter). The accompanying themes comprised the recognition of nationalist claims, the spread of democracy, free trade and a stress on moral leadership. Wilson declared:

> The question upon which the whole future peace and policy of the world depends is this: is the present war a struggle for a just and secure peace, or only for a new balance of power? If it be only a struggle for a new balance of power, who will guarantee, who can guarantee, the stable equilibrium of the new arrangement? Only a tranquil Europe can be a stable Europe. There must be, not a balance of power, but a community of power; not organized rivalries, but an organized common peace.[2]

The thwarting of these hopes by domestic opposition, European dictatorship and the failures of appeasement is a story with many historical interpretations. The standard contemporary account, associated especially with John Maynard Keynes and Walter Lippmann, stresses the doctrinaire character of Wilson's views and his incapacity relative to cannier French statesmen pursuing determinedly nationalistic agendas. The Versailles Treaty was, in Keynes's term, a Carthaginian Peace. This interpretation has been much challenged in recent years, with various scholars identifying in France a more moderate cast of mind, and in Britain a harsher one.

But of particular historical interest is the fate of Wilson's vision of the 'organized common peace'. To many of its liberal adherents, the idea of a community of power to restrain selfish and bellicose impulses became not collective resistance to aggression, but a euphemism for handing the problem to someone else.

27

## LIBERALISM ADRIFT

Sir Herbert Samuel was the principal spokesman for indifference to the demands of collective security. Partly this was personal. He had long shared the general mistrust among mainstream politicians of the mercurial talents of Winston Churchill. As early as 1933 he declared to the House of Commons that Churchill made:

> ...brilliant speeches on all subjects, but that is no reason why we should accept his political judgement. On the contrary, the brilliance of his speeches only makes the errors in his judgement the more conspicuous...I feel inclined to say of him what Bagehot said of another very distinguished Parliamentarian [Disraeli]: 'His chaff is excellent, but his wheat is poor stuff.'[3]

But more ominously, as the European dictators gave a foretaste of their foreign aggression by the way they treated domestic opponents, and two years after Japan's invasion of Manchuria in 1931, Samuel gave every indication of being uninterested in the substance, as opposed to the letter, of the Covenant of the League of Nations. He declared in favour of 'the continuous strengthening of the collective system of control – the active participation in international affairs through the League of Nations and the strengthening of the collective system'. Yet he did not will the means. He did not urge support for Article XVI of the League's Covenant, which pledged that an attack on one member state would be treated as an attack on all, and he explicitly rejected the notion of British participation in defensive collective action. In a speech to the House in July 1934, he asserted: 'The collective system must be really collective, and there is no reason why this country alone, or even with one or two sympathetic allies, should undertake obligations which really devolve upon humanity at large.'[4]

There was no such identifiable body as humanity at large, or at least none that could be held accountable for the failure of collective security. As the historian R. A. C. Parker observes of these sentiments: 'Support for the League became a disguise for isolation when its covenant was to be enforced by "humanity at large". Samuel, and the Liberals, seemed then to suppose that Britain could leave international problems to the League to solve.'[5]

The Liberal manifesto in the 1935 general election faithfully reflected such feelings. On the question of 'National Defence' it declared:

> Our aim is to maintain the peace of the world and preserve our own security. Armaments, on however vast a scale, will not bring security or stop war. The national defences must be kept efficient and large enough for the needs of the times, but a colossal, panic expenditure upon arms is not the road to peace. It is the duty of the House of Commons to examine, upon their merits and with the utmost care, all demands for increased expenditure, especially upon armaments, and to insist upon the strictest control of their manufacture and sale, and the elimination of the motive of private profit. It is the duty of the voters to elect a House of Commons that will do this. Through strengthening the League of Nations, and through international disarmament, and there alone, the true path to security lies.

In the year that Hitler announced German rearmament, in breach of the Versailles Treaty, and Mussolini invaded Abyssinia, the Liberals proposed controls on the manufacture of armaments and the elimination of the profit motive. They were not alone.

## LABOUR AND PACIFISM

Labour veered at the same time between obeisance to collective security and an embrace of outright pacifism. The official policy of the party was of support for the League and the Geneva Protocol. In 1928 the party asserted its 'whole-hearted support for the League of Nations as the arbiter of international peace and order, in preference to the basing of peace upon separate pacts, ententes and alliances'. Coercive action – by sanctions at least – was envisaged in order to deal with miscreant states. But the leading figures in the rump of the party that survived the election defeat of 1931 held distinctive – indeed highly idiosyncratic – versions of the party's message.

George Lansbury, Labour leader from 1931 to 1935, assumed that post in a fit of collective absent-mindedness, after Ramsay MacDonald (an underrated prime minister whose name even now is reviled within the Labour Party) went into coalition with the Conservatives. Lansbury's foreign policy in the age of the dictators was, literally, the Sermon on the Mount. He was an absolute pacifist whose contribution to political debate attracted much condescending tribute to his sincerity when what was required was brusque dismissal of his schemes.

It was a long time coming. Labour in fact passed unambiguously pacifist resolutions at its 1933 conference. One called for 'the total disarmament of all nations throughout the world and the creation of an International Police Force'. Another, carried unanimously, called on the party 'to pledge itself to take no part in war' and to decide with the trade union movement 'what steps, including a general strike, are to be taken to organise the opposition of the organised working-class movement in the event of war or threat of war'.[6]

The tenor of public debate in the mid-1930s was 'pacificist' (opposed to force as a means of settling international disputes, as opposed to a personal renunciation of it) and Labour was officially committed to the same principles. But pacifism (an absolutist refusal to engage in violence) went well beyond that. The most prominent peace-related activity of that time was the 'Peace Ballot' organised by the League of Nations Union in April 1934, in which eleven and a half million people took part. It recorded overwhelming support for security based on the League of Nations, and agreed disarmament among nations. But – however indefinitely extended it believed the scenario to be – it did reflect bare majority support for collective military action in the last resort.

The crucial question was: 'Do you consider that, if a nation insists on attacking another, the other nations should combine to compel it to stop by (a) economic and non-military measures? (b) if necessary, military measures?' To the first part of the question more than 90 per cent said 'yes'; to the second slightly over half said 'yes', and only 20 per cent said 'no'.[7]

## LABOUR AND COLLECTIVE SECURITY

Labour took tentative steps back to its declaratory policy of collective security in 1934, by reversing its vote of the previous year. The repression of the Austrian Socialists in the meantime had imbued Labour with a greater sense of reality about hostile forces in the international order. But the party remained powerfully influenced by two currents of anti-militarist thought. One was its pacifist wing. The other comprised adherents of the Hobson/Lenin thesis of the imperialist roots of war. These critics counterposed the interests of the international working-class movement to those of the arms manufacturers and profiteers. Most prominent among this second anti-war camp, which believed the League was a mere cover for the interests of imperialism, was Sir Stafford Cripps, described by Denis Healey (International Secretary of the Labour Party after the war, and Defence Secretary in the first Wilson Government) in his memoirs as 'a political ninny of a most superior quality'.[8] The particular incident that Healey alludes to is Cripps's opposition, on the eve of the Labour Party conference in 1936, to recruitment for the armed forces. Cripps insisted that a German war victory would matter little to British workers: 'British Fascism would be less brutal than German, but the world situation would be no better.'[9]

Labour's divisions over foreign policy became heated at the 1935 party conference, after Italy's invasion of Abyssinia. Ernest Bevin of the Transport and General Workers' Union, later Foreign Secretary in the Attlee Government, ridiculed Lansbury's devotion to diplomacy in preference to rearmament. Bevin denounced him for 'hawking your conscience round from body to body asking to be told what to do with it'. It was a mark of how unsuited to political office Lansbury was that he gave up the leadership without protest, and apparently without realising the extent of his humiliation.

Lansbury continued his efforts to resolve political tension by peaceful means, and thereby gave a valuable illustration of how the pursuit of diplomacy without the slightest awareness of its limits may become an *idée fixe*. In 1937 he travelled to the European capitals to propose a world congress to decide on the just distribution of world resources, and thereby supposedly remove the cause of war (a fallacy in thinking about international politics that has a long and undistinguished pedigree, and which is much heard in today's debates). Lansbury pronounced Hitler, who understandably gave him a sympathetic hearing, 'one of the great men of our time' and declared:

> [T]o live, Germany needs peace as much as any nation in the world. No one understands this better than Herr Hitler...When I came away [from meeting him] it was my sincere belief that if negotiations could be started at once accommodation might be found. The threat of war was only a silly illusion which would soon dissipate if I could arrange a meeting between Stalin, Hitler and Mussolini with somebody as chairman with a sense of humour... I feel that a pleasant day's conversation in a villa on the Riviera might bring these three statesmen to realise that they have...a world of peace and security to gain.[10]

Interestingly, the Italian aggression caused genuine outrage among the pro-League forces – as in principle it ought to have done, being a clear case of a unilateral and expansionist exercise of force – while the old balance-of-power school of British foreign policy proved compliant. As Michael Howard records, of these two voices – liberal internationalism and balance-of-power politics – 'it was the first, the voice of the liberal conscience, that now counselled war; the second, the voice of the government, the despised "establishment", that courted public and international humiliation to preserve peace'.[11]

## CONTRADICTORY IMPULSES AGAINST FASCISM AND WAR

This was the point at which a consistent commitment to collective security and the repulsion of aggression might have coalesced and been effective. It did not happen that way. Official policy completely misread Hitler's intentions, by which time public disquiet at the mishandling of Italy's aggression against Abyssinia (in which Sir Samuel Hoare had been forced to stand down as Foreign Secretary) had dissipated. The dominant sentiment had in fact become relief that every expedient was being taken to avert war by appeasing dictatorship.

The organised Left continued to be buffeted by its contradictory impulses to oppose both fascism and war, but Hitler's aggression in the Rhineland and the Spanish Civil War were brute facts that helped concentrate the mind. By 1937 Labour had belatedly realised that rearmament was essential to counter fascism, while the Conservatives rearmed but also attempted conciliation with Hitler. The much-depleted Liberal Party toughened its stance. Samuel had lost his seat in the 1935 election and had become Liberal leader in the Lords. The new party leader, Archibald Sinclair, sounded a note of conspicuous sense regarding Chamberlain's betrayal over the Sudetenland at Munich.

On Chamberlain's triumphant return from Munich, Sinclair issued a statement, noting that 'if war has been averted, peace has not yet been established. Immense sacrifices have been exacted from a small and weak nation; the freedom which hundreds of thousands of men and women now enjoy in the democracy of Czechoslovakia is to be surrendered to the German dictatorship at the bidding of the British and French governments.' He concluded by noting 'the failure of the policy of constant yielding to the threat of force'. The statement was carried in *The Times* ('The Destiny of Europe: Sir Archibald Sinclair's Unease') on 1 October 1938, and makes an instructive point of comparison with the newspaper's own leader ('A New Dawn'), which ventured: 'By [Hitler's] granting so much, the Czechs suffer no practical loss.'

One of the great polemics of twentieth-century British politics, *Guilty Men*,[12] written under the collective pseudonym

'Cato' by three left-wing journalists including the future Labour leader Michael Foot, cogently attacked the appeasement policies of the Conservatives, and noted the historic tragedy for Europe that a clear signal was not given to face down totalitarian expansionism. It was reticent on a matter of more parochial interest, but still of some importance. The historic tragedy for the Left was that it came to its own realisation of the futility of appeasement too late, its message being dissipated by supposedly progressive notions that were alternately reactionary and foolish.

## STALIN'S MACHINATIONS

Much confusion was sown, and persists to this day, about the association between the cause of democracy and interventionism because of the role of the Spanish Civil War. Fortunately, recent scholarship that makes use of the Soviet archives has injected clarity where previously there were educated guesses amid a hardy mythology. The standard left-wing anti-Communist view, much influenced by George Orwell's *Homage to Catalonia*, has always stressed the parasitic and brutal character of Stalin's intervention on the Republican side. The truth appears to be darker still: the standard account mischaracterises the non-Communist Left and underestimates the Comintern's direction of the Republican cause.

From 1933 the Spanish Socialists shifted fatefully towards a position termed by its advocates 'Bolshevisation'. Francisco Largo Caballero, former Labour Minister and future Prime Minister of a Popular Front Government, saw the Socialist Party as a revolutionary force quite distinct from its nominal counterparts – the British Labour Party and the French Socialists. In a speech delivered at the end of 1933, he stated that 'the difference between [the Communists] and us is no more than words'.[13] Though the Leninist trend in the party had its internal critics, the Socialists issued a ten-point revolutionary programme in 1934 that presupposed revolutionary change. The programme proposed the dissolution of religious orders and the expropriation of their property, dissolution of the Civil Guard and the abolition of the army, to be replaced by a workers' militia. The leader of the party's youth wing, Carlos Hernández, called for a 'revolutionary purification' of the party and 'the reconstruction of the international worker movement on the basis of the Russian Revolution!'[14] The Spanish Socialists' politics were those of the street rather than the democratic trade union and labour movement.

Further, we know from the Soviet archives the extent of Stalin's control of the Republican cause, as well as his embezzlement of it and his suppression of its non-Communist elements. The 42,000-strong International Brigade was under the command not of a Canadian volunteer, as was the official story, but of a Soviet Commissar, Manfred Stern. Franco's was a vicious, clerical-reactionary despotism, but with regionally circumscribed significance. Conversely, a Republican victory would probably have meant an outpost of Stalin's foreign policy – which was far from being an anti-fascist force, and was determinedly expansionist. As Antony Beevor, in a recent review article, has noted:

> There is nothing in any recent book on the subject to soften the cold brutality of the Nationalists...But more than enough has emerged to confirm that all those who went to fight on behalf of the Republic in the cause of freedom were completely duped.[15]

The European democracies have received, with good reason, much obloquy for their failure to take effective measures against fascism in the 1930s. But one of the most frequently cited charges – the abandonment of Spanish Republican democracy – has served principally to deflect genuine historical accountability. Only once the Spanish Civil War became unwinnable did Stalin loosen his grip on the Republican cause, which – contrary to a simplistic explanation merely of Stalinist betrayal – itself had long since abandoned democracy. In short, and with great relevance for future debates on the Left, the notion that the Soviet Union, for all its domestic repression, was – or could possibly be – an ally in the cause of peace was wrong. So far from being a force for the defence of popular

government against aggression, the Soviet Union was an imperialist power as brutal in its foreign conduct as in its domestic
repression.

## TOTALITARIANISM: THREE HERETICAL RESPONSES

There was a final set of allied responses on the Left and in the
peace movement to the issues of totalitarianism and national
security, and these were the most unsettling of all tendencies so
far discussed. The mildest of these three positions was a devotion to the cause of peace so single-minded that it overlooked
the evils of fascism. Beyond this, a more extreme tendency
actively romanticised fascism. Finally came a third position
that explicitly identified with Britain's totalitarian enemies.

The principal culprit among the advocates of the first position was the Peace Pledge Union (PPU). This venerable pacifist
organisation grew from a letter to the *Manchester Guardian*
in October 1934 from an Anglican clergyman, Canon Dick
Sheppard, denouncing war. Sheppard received huge public support for his views. A mass movement speedily arose. As with
the temperance movement, whose ethos the PPU resembled,
members signed a pledge – in this case reading: 'I renounce
war, and I will never support or sanction another.' Predictably,
the movement never regained such levels of support after it
became clear to all but the most fervent of Canon Sheppard's
flock that a pledge against war was ineffective against aggressive tyrannies that unaccountably declined to be held to the
same standard.[16]

Even after the outbreak of war, the PPU went beyond an
ethical conviction to a perverse utilitarian calculus. John
Middleton Murry wrote in the PPU's journal, *Peace News* (of
which he was editor), on 9 August 1940: 'Personally I don't
believe that a Hitlerian Europe would be quite so terrible as
most people believe it would be.'[17]

Murry at least had the belated sense eventually to
acknowledge the moral failings of pacifism as a counter to
Nazi aggression and genocide. (He is now best remembered as
a literary critic and editor of the peerless short stories of his
late wife, Katherine Mansfield.) The same could not be said of

the best known of all pacifist campaigners, Vera Brittain, author of some forgettable novels but also of the moving auto-biographical *Testament of Youth*. In one of her regular letters to her fellow-campaigners, on 3 May 1945, she maintained that the gas chambers were being publicised by the allies 'partly, at least, in order to divert attention from the havoc produced in German cities by allied obliteration bombing'.[18]

Thus did an ethical objection to war – misguided, but not inherently ignoble – become a position indifferent to tyranny and genocide. But that was not the worst of it. George Orwell – who snapped out of his own anti-war illusions quickly enough once war was declared – wrote of this tendency in his essay 'Notes on Nationalism' in May 1945:

> The majority of pacifists either belong to obscure religious sects or are simply humanitarians who object to the taking of life and prefer not to follow their thoughts beyond that point. But there is a minority of intellectual pacifists whose real though unadmitted motive appears to be hatred of western democracy and admiration of totalitarianism...

> Pacifist literature abounds with equivocal remarks which, if they mean anything, appear to mean that statesmen of the type of Hitler are preferable to those of the type of Churchill, and that violence is perhaps excusable if it is violent enough. After the fall of France, the French pacifists, faced by a real choice which their English colleagues have not had to make, mostly went over to the Nazis, and in England there appears to have been some small overlap of membership between the Peace Pledge Union and the Blackshirts [the colloquial name for Sir Oswald Mosley's British Union of Fascists (BUF)].[19]

Despite his harsh words about pacifists, and despite peace campaigners' outrage then and now against him, Orwell was not overstating his case. It is true that the overlap between membership of the Peace Pledge Union and the Blackshirts was numerically small. The personalities involved in pro-Nazi

activity by British pacifists were, however, by no means inci-
dental to the organised peace movement, and the activity itself
took place in organisations other than Mosley's BUF. A recent
insight into these connections has been provided by Sir Ian
Kershaw, the renowned biographer of Hitler, in a study of a
minor Conservative politician, Lord Londonderry. Londonderry became convinced in the 1930s of the necessity of
improving relations with Germany in order to avoid war.[20] It
was a distinctively aristocratic sentiment that differed from the
outright expressions of pro-Nazism and anti-Semitism that
could be found among other appeasers, including those in
Londonderry's own party. But there was a link between these
groups, formalised in an organisation called, appropriately,
'The Link'. Kershaw notes that this organisation, while ostensibly calling for better international relations, was also 'heavily
laced with anti-Semitism and fervent support for Nazism'.[21]

Londonderry – stupid rather than malign, but *very* stupid
– decided that, though The Link was indeed pro-Nazi, he
shared its judgement that Munich represented a reasonable
resolution of justified German complaints. He thus added his
name to a letter to the then house organ of appeasement, *The
Times* (12 October 1938), to that effect, along with half a
dozen council members of The Link and various other Nazi
sympathisers. His reputation never recovered.

One person who, unlike Londonderry, did hold membership of The Link was Canon Stuart Morris, who had succeed-
ed Dick Sheppard as Chairman of the PPU. Another leading
member of the PPU, the Marquess of Tavistock (later the Duke
of Bedford) founded an explicitly pro-Nazi and anti-Semitic
party in April 1939, the British People's Party (BPP). The
party's treasurer, Ben Greene, a former Labour Party candidate, was also a member of the PPU, which helped him to
establish a periodical that freely lifted material from pro-Nazi
sources. The PPU executive eventually expressed some disquiet
at – though scarcely opposition to – the slant Greene was
adopting, but leading PPU members continued to support the
Nazi cause. The BPP fought a by-election in Hythe shortly
after its formation; a prominent speaker in support of its can-

didate was yet another leading pacifist campaigner, Dr Maude Royden. (In a neat historical irony, the candidate was the explorer St John Philby, father of Kim Philby; admiration for totalitarianism was clearly a family trait.) Dr Royden continued to support the BPP before and after the outbreak of war.[22]

Right up until 1943, the Marquess of Tavistock sat on the national council of the PPU. He was nominated also the following year but declined to serve. In *Peace News* (30 October 1942), he invoked the following rationalisation for Nazi aggression in Europe:

> ...the very serious provocation which many Jews have given by their avarice and arrogance when exploiting Germany's financial difficulties, by their associations with commercialized vice, and by their monopolization of certain professions.[23]

### THE LEFT'S RESPONSIBILITY

To sum up: as Great Britain entered and fought a war to defeat barbarism, the Left could only reflect on its own share of responsibility for the absence of a reputable alternative to appeasement. Balance-of-power politics had proved not only attenuated in vision but also incapable of realising its own stated goals. Yet any genuine commitment to collective security to resist aggression had been undermined by three distinct heresies among liberals and left-wingers.

First, a pacifism rooted in the Nonconformist Churches' personal moralism was widely observed within the labour movement. (The puritanical character of this tradition was epitomised in a blithe assertion by Lansbury, himself an Anglican: 'It is...quite certain that in Socialist England there will be no "pubs" as we know them today.'[24]) Secondly, a conviction that fascism was but a form of capitalism and imperialism, which remained the real enemy, was not only a gross political misreading of the distinction between totalitarianism and constitutional democracy, but also a means of denigrating one's own society. Thirdly, a professed commitment to collective security through the League of Nations in some cases

disguised an isolationism determined to leave the task of policing an anarchic international order to others. On the fringes of
the peace movement, this became indistinguishable from outright sympathy for totalitarianism.

All of these variants of left-wing response to the gathering
storm of the totalitarian expansionism of the Axis powers
were to prove durable, even after their signal refutation.

1 Quoted in Michael Mandelbaum, *The Ideas that Conquered the World*
(Cambridge, MA: Perseus Books, 2002), p. 404. This and the previous
paragraph draw on Mandelbaum's account of Wilson's domestic debates
over the League of Nations.
2 Wilson to the Senate, 22 January 1917, quoted in Tony Smith,
*America's Mission* (Princeton: Princeton University Press, 1994), p. 94.
3 Quoted in David Cannadine, *In Churchill's Shadow* (London: Allen
Lane, 2002), p. 103
4 Quoted in R. A. C. Parker, *Chamberlain and Appeasement*
(Basingstoke: Macmillan, 1993), p. 308.
5 *Ibid.* p. 308.
6 Quoted in Rhiannon Vickers, *The Labour Party and the World:
The Evolution of Labour's Foreign Policy, 1900–51* (Manchester:
Manchester University Press, 2003), pp. 109–10.
7 Michael Howard, *War and the Liberal Conscience* (Oxford: Oxford
University Press, 1978), pp. 87–8.
8 Denis Healey, *The Time of My Life* (London: Michael Joseph, 1989),
p. 479.
9 Quoted in Vickers, *The Labour Party and the World*, p. 118.
10 George Lansbury, *My Quest for Peace* (1938); quoted in Parker,
*Chamberlain and Appeasement*, p. 310.
11 Howard, *War and the Liberal Conscience*, p. 94.
12 'Cato', *Guilty Men* (London: Victor Gollancz, 1940)
13 Quoted in Stanley G. Payne, *The Spanish Civil War, the Soviet Union,
and Communism* (New Haven: Yale University Press, 2004), p. 46.
This paragraph draws heavily on Payne's important book.
14 Quoted in Payne, *Ibid.* p. 70.
15 Antony Beevor, 'Who started the Spanish Civil War?', *Times Literary
Supplement*, 9 March 2005. Beevor's judgement might be thought a
sweeping generalisation, but the evidence is that even the reputable
elements of the Republican cause were useless so far as an effective
opposition to European fascism was concerned. As late as March 1939,

George Orwell was urging a revolt against war with Germany. In a letter to the art critic Herbert Read he envisaged that the revolt would 'form itself into two sections, that of the dissident lefts like ourselves, and that of the fascists, this time the idealistic Hitler-fascists, in England more or less represented by [Sir Oswald] Mosley. I don't know whether Mosley will have the sense and guts to stick out against war with Germany, he might decide to cash in on the patriotism business, but in that case something else will take his place.' (Letter to Herbert Read, in *The Collected Essays, Journalism and Letters of George Orwell*, ed. Ian Angus and Sonia Orwell [London: Penguin, 1968], Volume 1, p. 425.)

16 Sheppard died in 1937, and thus did not live to witness the dashing of his ideals. Shortly before his death, however, he expressed his hopes in a speech that suggested they could survive a fair degree of dashing: 'Last night I had a dream. In it George Lansbury and I were playing tennis against Hitler and Mussolini. George had a game leg and I was asthmatic but we won six-love' (quoted in Adrian Hastings, *A History of English Christianity, 1920–2000* [London: SCM Press, 2001], p.333). There is a portrait of Sheppard on the west wall of the magnificent Church of St Martin-in-the-Fields; he looks appropriately cherubic.

17 Quoted in Martin Ceadel, *Semi-Detached Idealists: The British Peace Movement and International Relations, 1854–1945* (Oxford: Oxford University Press, 2000), p. 421.

18 *Ibid.* p. 422.

19 George Orwell, 'Notes on Nationalism', in *The Collected Essays*, Volume 3, pp. 424–5. This passage has become quite well known and widely cited since 9/11 in opposition to the modern anti-war movement. It has always been a sentiment that Orwell's detractors, notably Raymond Williams and more recently Scott Lucas, find offensive. Christopher Hitchens also cites the passage in his book *Orwell's Victory* (London: Allen Lane, 2002), p. 9, but makes a transcription error: Orwell referred to the pacifists' 'unadmitted motive', which Hitchens renders as 'unacknowledged motive'. 'Unadmitted', with its implication of concealment, is the better word.

20 Ian Kershaw, *Making Friends with Hitler* (London: Allen Lane, 2004).

21 *Ibid.* p. 247.

22 See Richard Griffiths, *Patriotism Perverted: Captain Ramsay, the Right Club and Antisemitism, 1939–40* (London: Constable and Robinson, 1998). Ramsay was a fiercely anti-Semitic Tory MP who was interned for his pro-Nazi sympathies. His Right Club was an organisation that we may assume would have furnished a Vichy-type regime had the

Nazis conquered Britain. For many years the membership book of the Club was believed lost, but it resurfaced in a solicitor's office in 1990.

23 Quoted in Ceadel, *Semi-Detached Idealists*, p. 413.

24 Quoted in Jose Harris, 'Labour's political and social thought', in D. Tanner, P. Thane and N. Tiratsoo (eds), *Labour's First Century* (Cambridge: Cambridge University Press, 2000), p. 22.

# CHAPTER 2

# THE LEFT AND THE COLD WARS

*It is given to few men to see their dreams fulfilled.*
*Three times in the last year I know I have nearly died,*
*but I have kept myself alive because I wanted to see*
*the Atlantic Alliance properly launched.*
*This has been done today.*
Ernest Bevin, April 1949

## CONFRONTING THE SOVIET UNION

For all its flaws, errors, defeats and disasters, the Labour Party has done important and admirable things in foreign policy. The most historically significant was its role in the early Cold War. This was not foreordained. Labour leader Clement Attlee bolstered the cause of collective security in the late 1930s and served patriotically in the wartime coalition. Yet in theory he was convinced that socialist ideology trumped mere national interest in foreign policy. In his 1937 credo *The Labour Party in Perspective* (still much cited by left-wingers impressed with its premise that a sufficiently bold socialist government can legislate away entrenched interests), he insisted:

> First it must be perfectly clear that the Labour Party rejects altogether the theory that foreign policy is something that must be kept out of party politics. It does not agree that there is some policy to be pursued by this country irrespective of what party is in power, a policy which is national and so transcends party differences. There is a deep difference of opinions between the Labour Party and the Capitalist parties on foreign as well as home policy, because the two cannot be separated. The foreign policy of a government is the reflection of its internal policy.[1]

Attlee allowed that blanket opposition to the foreign policies of a capitalist government was 'stupid', but insisted that 'particular instances of action which can be approved by Socialists do not affect the truth that there is no agreement on foreign policy between a Labour Opposition and a Capitalist government'.[2]

In fact, Labour's foreign policy was derivative not of its home policy but of its ideology. Acknowledging that the Soviet Union posed the gravest threat to free trade unionism and social democracy, Labour adopted – in the words of the standard history of the Attlee Governments – an 'unrelenting hostility towards the Soviet Union [that] led in time to a new relationship between Britain and the United States'.[3]

Labour came to office in 1945 believing that it was well placed to cultivate good relations with the Soviet Union. The common belief that Ernest Bevin, Attlee's Foreign Secretary, had approvingly pronounced that 'Left understands Left' is not strictly correct – Bevin had in fact been referring to France rather than to any claim on Labour's part to a greater facility for accommodation with the Soviet Union. But it is true that, just as there was on the Left in the 1930s a widely shared Marxist analysis of the wastefulness and bellicosity of capitalism, so it was expected there would be some congruence of view between a Labour Government and the Soviet Union.

This turned out to be not the case at all, because of Soviet actions, which were hostile to the institutions of liberal democracy, and especially to parties of the democratic Left. Labour – the strongest such party in Europe at the time – gave historically vital aid to other social democratic parties and free trade unions on both sides of the Iron Curtain to resist Communist infiltration and expansionism. (The author of this policy was Bevin's protégé Denis Healey – not yet an MP but International Secretary of the Labour Party.) It was a natural development of Labour's democratic socialism to support the Brussels Treaty in 1948, which committed British troops to remain in Germany for 15 years, and which was intended to serve as a stimulus for the United States to commit itself to the defence of Western Europe. So it did. Labour was thereby instrumental in the founding of Nato in 1949 – a voluntary alliance establishing collective security and deterrence, which 40 years later, with the collapse of Communism in Eastern Europe, became the most successful liberation movement in history.

Bevin's tenure at the Foreign Office involved a delicate balance of trying to entrench the United States in the security of Western Europe while dispensing with foreign commitments that Britain could not undertake on its own. The decision to develop an independent nuclear deterrent needs to be seen in this context. It was not clear in 1946 that the US would necessarily commit itself to the defence of Western Europe. As Attlee later remarked:

> If we had decided not to have it, we would have put
> ourselves entirely in the hands of the Americans.
> That would have been to take a risk a British government
> should not take. It's all very well to look back and say
> otherwise, but at the time nobody could be sure that the
> Americans would not revert to isolationism – many
> Americans wanted it, many Americans feared it.
> There was no Nato then.[4]

The decision, communicated to the State Department in February 1947, to remove troops from Greece and Turkey and end economic assistance to both countries from the end of the following month had comparable motivations. It was inevitable given Britain's straitened economic circumstances, and it had the desired effect of stimulating an assessment of policy by the Truman Administration. That policy came to be known as the Truman Doctrine. Nearly 60 years later the Truman Doctrine still stands as a model for progressive thinking, yet it was grounded in the conviction that totalitarianism was a threat to peace as well as a moral abomination. It was laid out on 12 March 1947 by President Truman in an address to Congress:

To ensure the peaceful development of nations, free from coercion, the United States has taken a leading part in establishing the United Nations...We shall not realize our objectives, however, unless we are willing to help free peoples to maintain their free institutions and their national integrity against aggressive movements that seek to impose upon them totalitarian regimes. This is no more than a frank recognition that totalitarian regimes imposed on free peoples, by direct or indirect aggression, undermine the foundations of international peace and hence the security of the United States.

Excepting Cyprus, the US assumed what had been British responsibilities in the Eastern Mediterranean, and carried them out with a fair degree of success. (In this it was assisted by fissures within the Communist movement. The Greek Communists became isolated and were eventually defeated as they lost the backing of Yugoslavia under Tito.) It also, in June 1947, committed itself to the reconstruction of Europe with Marshall Aid. In September the Communist putsch in Czechoslovakia demonstrated an altogether different mode of relations between states on either side of the Iron Curtain.

### THE LEFT AND BEVIN

Post-war debate on the Left about foreign policy was marked by a widespread disillusion with the supposedly pacific intentions of the Soviet Union. The evidence unequivocally supported Bevin's approach. While there was a body of opinion within the Labour Party that was unabashedly pro-Soviet, its numbers were small and the support for Bevin's approach was perhaps surprisingly broad. Only later did the pro-Soviet and neutralist camps within the party become influential.

Dissent centred on the Keep Left group of MPs, whose inspiration was the pamphlet *Keep Left* published in May 1947; its authors were Richard Crossman, Michael Foot and Ian Mikardo. The argument was a fairly standard call for a progressive third force in foreign policy between the Soviet Union and the capitalist USA, but it was careful to avoid language that might be interpreted as sympathetic to the Soviets. (Labour had already not only forcefully rejected affiliation by the Communist Party, but proscribed dual membership of the Labour Party with any organisation having its own programme and principles 'or owing any allegiance to any organisation abroad' – in this case, the Comintern and its successor organisation the Cominform, created in 1947.)

Almost as soon as it had been issued, that argument was refuted by events. The announcement in the summer of 1947 of Marshall Aid for the reconstruction of Western Europe, coupled with the Soviet Union's refusal to take part itself in the scheme, undercut the parliamentary opposition to Bevin's foreign policies. Opposition was confined to a tiny caucus of Labour MPs, whom the party expelled from membership or otherwise withheld support from.

One of these, John Platts-Mills QC, died only in 2001, aged 95. He was so shameless an apologist for Stalin that even an obsequious *Guardian* obituary could scarcely overlook his record. It compromised by imputing to him values lodged somewhere in his psyche that were somehow absent from his political record: 'He seemed to visit and support every Warsaw Pact country – though, as a true freedom-lover at heart, he could not accept the invasions of Czechoslovakia and Hungary.'[5]

But a more influential force over the longer term was Konni Zilliacus, MP for Gateshead. The reputation of Zilliacus (his unusual name was of Swedo-Finnish origin; he was determinedly cosmopolitan and an accomplished linguist) was restored to some extent by his reinstatement in the party some years later and his service thereafter as Labour MP for Manchester Gorton. But a determined effort at rehabilitation came in 2002 with the publication of a hagiography by a writer who is described as a moderator in history courses for the North East Open College Network.[6] This unremittingly disgusting book is distinguished only by its judicious omission of the most interesting fact about its subject's political agitation: he was the rhetorical peg on which George Orwell hung his criticism of the Tribune Left in the late 1940s for its failure to acknowledge the futility of pressing for an independent socialist foreign policy for Europe.

Orwell entitled his essay, with heavy irony, 'In Defence of Comrade Zilliacus'. His point was that Zilliacus was at least *openly* pro-Soviet, whereas the Tribune Left knew that that was a disreputable position but was reluctant to say so publicly. Orwell observed:

> We are no longer strong enough to stand alone, and if we fail to bring a western European union into being, we shall be obliged, in the long run, to subordinate our policy to that of one Great Power or the other. And in spite of all the fashionable chatter of the moment, everyone knows in his heart that we should choose America. The great mass of people in this country would, I believe, make this choice almost instinctively. Certainly there is a small minority that would choose the other side. Mr Zilliacus, for instance, is one of them. I think he is wrong, but at least he makes his position clear. I also know perfectly well what *Tribune*'s position is. But has *Tribune* ever made it clear?[7]

Zilliacus's biography carries a preface by Tony Benn, who declares the book 'a brilliant biography of a brilliant man' – but more significant is Benn's judgement of the Attlee Government (to which the present Government is often unfavourably compared by stalwarts of 'Old Labour'):

> Unfortunately the post-war Labour government whose record is now widely recognised as having been a brilliant story of progressive reform was marred by its subservience to Washington and its deep hostility to the USSR for which Ernie Bevin must take some responsibility, and criticism of this policy in the House of Commons led to Zilly's own expulsion.

In a perfect symbiosis of prefacer, author and subject, the whole book is as shameless as this. It quotes Zilliacus's defence – his *defence*, in a letter to *Tribune* – of the coup in Czechoslovakia:

The Czechoslovak workers acting pretty much unanimously through the trade unions and the Social Democratic as well as the Communist Party made a bloodless semi-revolution rather than allow the Right and centre to get away with their avowed object in bringing down the Government and forcing an anti-Communist coalition on the model of what has happened in France and Italy.[8]

All that his biographer can say of Zilliacus's support for the overthrow of parliamentary government is: 'Very few people in the Labour Party agreed with Zilliacus on this point...' And by the standards of this book, that is as far as indictment goes.

The indictment is, however, quite true. Very few people in the Labour Party at that time were willing to associate with Zilliacus's pro-Sovietism. Zilliacus's biographer makes the disingenuous argument that what appeared to be a pro-Soviet stance was in fact more heterodox than it appeared, being pro-Tito rather than pro-Stalin. But the language and stance of Zilliacus's part of the Left mirrored precisely the line of the Communist Party of Great Britain.

Zilliacus wrote to Attlee on 11 February 1946 at inordinate length (and made a virtue of verbosity by terming his remarks a memorandum) to condemn 'the foreign policy they [the Government] inherited from the Tories'. He concluded: 'Stop preparations for possible war against the USSR and join with fellow members of the Security Council to form an international police force and joint use of national forces.'[9] A contemporary Communist tract entitled *Mr Bevin's Record* by the Stalinist ideologue R. Palme Dutt said much the same, declaring that 'the gravest charge of all is the betrayal of peace by Mr Bevin's policy and the rising menace of a new world war'. According to Dutt's stilted and enervating prose:

The aggressive war aims of the American militarists and their Anglo-American War Bloc are openly proclaimed. They are the aims of Churchill's Fulton speech.

Their entire strategy is directed to preparing a world war against the Socialist Soviet Union and the freedom of the peoples everywhere.[10]

In summary, the Attlee Government's support for the Truman Doctrine represents a peculiarly important phenomenon in the history of the British and European Left. The defence of democracy overseas was a cause that Labour devoted itself to, and in many respects played an essential role in supporting. It cemented the disillusionment of the democratic Left with the romantic notion that divisions on the Left represented a continuum of greater or lesser degrees of radicalism, rather than an unbridgeable gulf between the proponents of an open society and those who served as either advocates of or apologists for totalitarianism. A fierce determination to police the boundary between democratic socialism and Communism was grounded in direct experience of Communist methods on both sides of the Iron Curtain in undermining free trade unions and the labour movement.

Allying with the leading capitalist democracy did not come instinctively to Labour. It came instead through experience: the overwhelming evidence presented by the Soviet blockade of Berlin, eschewal of the cause of reconstruction of Europe, and repression of the satellite states of Eastern Europe. It was confirmed towards the end of Attlee's Government by the direct Communist aggression that sparked the Korean War.

Through all this, however, there remained pockets of strong dissent on the Left towards Atlanticist policies from those who favoured an independent and non-aligned foreign policy. There was also a durable pro-Communist element in the labour and trade union movement. At first insignificant, both of these currents in the labour movement gained strength as memories of the early Cold War receded. They required, though did not altogether receive, a reassessment by the democratic Left of how best to entrench a coalition in support of the defence of the Western democracies.

## REJECTION OF A TRADITION

At what point the degeneration of the European left-wing tradition of militant anti-totalitarianism set in is debatable. It involved, however, more than merely a shift in defence policies from hawkish to dovish. It represented a reassessment of the forces of totalitarianism – from a reliable anti-Communism combined with a belief in domestic reform, to a reflexive anti-Americanism.

It was most obvious in the British Labour Party's abandonment of its Cold War traditions to join the anti-nuclear campaigns of the 1980s. It was also apparent much earlier, however, in the German Social Democrats' resiling from their own anti-Communism to favour direct negotiations with East Germany. Other examples were the Swedish Social Democrats' transition from Erlander to Palme; and the similar trajectory of the Socialist International, under Braunthal and Brouckere, to the unthinking anti-anti-Communism that supported totalitarian movements in the Third World. At the same time, similar sentiments arose in US liberalism, in which the liberal anti-totalitarianism associated with such figures as Senator Henry Jackson became little more than a ginger group within a party that a generation earlier had been that tradition's most effective exponent.

## A GERMAN AUGURY

The relapse of the social democratic Left into pacificism was – with the important exception of France, devoted to its Gaullist conception of an independent nuclear *force de frappe* – a phenomenon that crossed Western Europe in the early 1980s. No party suffered more from this tendency than the British Labour Party, but an augury was provided by the German Social Democrats (SPD), under Willy Brandt, Chancellor from 1969 to 1973.

Brandt's early political activity – before, during and after the war, when contending with different types of totalitarianism – was little short of heroic. As Mayor of West Berlin from 1957 to 1968 he represented a free city cruelly divided by totalitarianism and by a Wall built to incarcerate East Germans.

Brandt's service as Chancellor was less distinguished. He was motivated by a commendable concern for his 17 million compatriots in the prison-state of East Germany, but his desire for German unity overcame the shared premises of Christian Democrats and Social Democrats that had been established after the war. Whereas German conservatism had historically been authoritarian, xenophobic and nationalist, Christian Democracy after the war – under the leadership of Konrad Adenauer – became liberal and pro-Western. The Social Democrats, while nominally (till the Bad Godesberg Conference of 1959) a Marxist party that had initially opposed Adenauer's Atlanticism, was staunchly anti-Communist under the leadership of Kurt Schumacher.

Brandt shifted that emphasis. Instead of contrasting the free West with the totalitarian East, as Adenauer did, or locating the threat to progressive values in Soviet imperialism, as Schumacher did, Brandt anticipated the language of the European Nuclear Disarmament Campaign a decade later. He spoke of the artificial division of Europe, which he hoped to overcome through his *Neue Ostpolitik*. Brandt put his faith not in military deterrence, but in the erosion of mistrust. As Chancellor he made it clear that West Germany's security was grounded in the Atlantic Alliance, and he famously – and movingly – knelt before the memorial to the Warsaw Ghetto, in expiation of his country's recent barbaric past. Yet he never once called directly for the defeat of Communism in the way that his SPD predecessors had. His ally and negotiator Egon Bahr argued for *Koexistenz auf deutsch* – or a specifically German form of co-existence between the divided parts of Europe – rather than a common Western policy grounded in a shared commitment to liberal-democratic values.

## SPLITS ON THE LEFT

This issue goes to the heart of the split that occurred in the European and American Left in the 1970s and 1980s. The older liberal and social democratic tradition – that of Attlee, Bevin, Schumacher and Truman – was instinctively anti-Communist. It knew that liberalism and social democracy were Communism's worst enemies. Gradually that understanding gave way to the notion that the Cold War was an artificial division born of mistrust rather than, as it was, a reflection of irrevocable political differences.

For a few years the extent of the shift was obscured by the experience of government. The Social Democrats in coalition government in Germany governed quite effectively. As Chancellor from 1976 to 1982, Helmut Schmidt presided over economic stability, cracked down on the terrorist Red Army Fraction, and conducted a far-sighted international policy. He perceived that the Soviet deployment of intermediate-range missiles in Europe threatened the credibility of a Western policy of extended deterrence. The gap in Western capabilities had to be filled by the deployment of Cruise and Pershing missiles – a historic Nato decision that galvanised the peace movement but proved invaluable in convincing the Soviet Union that it would be unable to win a nuclear arms race.

Indeed European leadership within Nato showed appreciably more resolve than the US administration of the time. A feckless and vacillating US President with minimal experience in international affairs, Jimmy Carter first secured the agreement of Schmidt and British Prime Minister James Callaghan to the deployment of the neutron bomb to counter Soviet intermediate-range missiles, and then in 1978 decided against that deployment. This reversal damaged the cohesion of Nato. It took largeness of character on the part of Europe's two most prominent social democratic leaders to face down their own parties and then to continue working effectively with the White House when their positions had been undermined.

Both men became prophets without honour on the European Left in the 1980s, which rejected Nato's twin-track strategy of deploying euromissiles while negotiating on arms control. Callaghan became a particular figure of obloquy for secretly continuing with the modernisation of Britain's Polaris fleet and preparing for its eventual replacement by a new generation of nuclear weapons, the American submarine-launched Trident system, in defiance of the views of the Labour Party conference.

## THE EUROMISSILE CONTROVERSY

European opposition to Nato strategy in the early 1980s reflected a curious belief – reinforced by loose talk from a new President, Ronald Reagan – that a new generation of intermediate-range missiles was being deployed in order to fight a 'limited' nuclear war in Europe. The notion was preposterous. The rationale of Nato's deployment was the opposite. Schmidt himself was regarded as the begetter of this deployment, in a speech he gave to the International Institute of Strategic Studies in 1977. In it, he worried publicly about the credibility of extended deterrence in Europe when the Soviet Union was deploying its own new intermediate-range missiles, the SS-4s and SS-5s. Nato's purpose was to tie the United States to the defence of Western Europe. If the Soviets threatened to use missiles in the European 'theatre', and Nato had no weapons of comparable range but only the US strategic nuclear arsenal with which to retaliate, then they might calculate that the US would be deterred from retaliating. In short, deterrence might fail because of a gap in the system of extended deterrence on which Nato strategy rested.

Cruise and Pershing II missiles were intended to resolve this problem, by providing the US with more options than just the strategic nuclear arsenal in the event of Soviet aggression. With the deployment of Nato's euromissiles, a Soviet nuclear threat would be less credible. A so-called limited nuclear war became less likely with a strengthening of deterrence and the reaffirmation of the US commitment to Europe's defence. But the peace movement maintained the opposite, completely misunderstanding Cruise and Pershing as a means for the US to avoid becoming embroiled in a strategic nuclear war.

Hundreds of thousands of demonstrators thus filled the streets of European capital cities in the early 1980s because of a mistake. The campaign against the euromissiles reinvigorated the Campaign for Nuclear Disarmament (CND), once famous for its Easter Aldermaston marches, but which had stagnated and then declined after the Partial Test Ban Treaty of 1963. Ominously, it won substantial constituency and parliamentary support within the Labour Party, after the party's defeat in the 1979 election. Denis Healey, former Cold Warrior and Defence Secretary in the 1964–70 Labour Government, was defeated in the election for Labour leader in 1980 on the resignation of James Callaghan – by, of all people, the veteran CND campaigner Michael Foot. Foot then presided over Labour's worst schism and greatest electoral humiliation since the 1930s.

Michael Foot is now regarded with the universal affection that is the privilege of advanced age, so it is especially worth recalling his record of political incompetence. Circumlocutory in argument, incoherent in exposition, almost entirely unfamiliar with economics, and – throughout all his tribulations – convinced of his place in history, he has never realised that the critical pasting he received as Labour leader was still more restrained than he had any right to expect. To describe Labour's 1983 general election manifesto as the longest suicide note in history is kindness itself to a programme simultaneously Procrustean, doctrinaire and isolationist, founded on the twin themes of economic *dirigisme* and unilateral nuclear disarmament. It scarcely does justice to the determined unreality of such assertions as: 'Labour believes that Ireland should, by peaceful means and on the basis of consent, be united, and recognises that this will be achieved with the introduction of socialist policies.'

But the oddity of Labour's election campaign on defence was that, while being anti-nuclear, it was also ruinously contradictory. To propitiate Healey and other Atlanticists, the manifesto deliberately obscured the obvious question of whether Britain would give up its Polaris fleet even if it received no matching reductions from the Soviet Union. (Even then, the obvious question was disingenuous, because the Soviet Union could not match the removal of Britain's entire nuclear arsenal without itself becoming a non-nuclear power.)

Amid this confusion, in a campaign already doomed, James Callaghan helpfully gave a speech – which he made sure was televised – rejecting Labour's disarmament policies. Callaghan stated forcefully that those policies were out of line with the party's traditional stance and that he did not support them. At least one Labour MP – John Gilbert, who eventually returned to government as a defence minister after Tony Blair's first election victory – was convinced that he held his marginal seat only because Callaghan had spoken out. Predictably, Callaghan was castigated by more frenetic members of the Labour Party ('Guilty Men' ran the headline in the post-election issue of *Tribune*, in an obvious and offensive allusion to the pre-war appeasers) but he was talking sense. At that year's party conference, to a chorus of boos from constituency delegates, he stated the issue matter-of-factly:

> What the movement has failed to understand is that it reversed the traditional policy of the Labour Party on which we had fought 11 successive elections without any real attempt to convince the British people that what we were doing was right. I happen to believe it is wrong. But you make a fundamental mistake by believing that by going on marches and passing resolutions without any attempt to try to tell the British people what the consequences were, you could carry their vote. *And you lost millions of votes.*[11]

On that last sentence, Callaghan was drowned out by opposing cries from constituency activists of '*you* did' – it was the temper of the times. Yet what was overlooked in these post-election recriminations was that, by its very incoherence, Labour was not formally committed to the full unilateralist catechism of CND in 1983. That happened only a year later, with Labour's new defence programme of 1984 (*Defence and Security for Britain*), under the leadership of Neil Kinnock. This did commit the party to the unilateral abandonment of Britain's existing nuclear deterrent, along with the cancellation of Trident, the sending back of Cruise missiles (which had been deployed in 1983), and the closure of all US nuclear bases in Britain. It was extraordinary that Denis Healey, then Labour's Shadow Foreign Secretary, publicly reconciled himself to this programme, but not as extraordinary as the widespread impression that Labour became marginally more moderate in these barren years. On defence, it in fact became still more extreme. Kinnock only finally abandoned unilateral nuclear disarmament in 1989, once the defence issue had lost much of its salience owing to factors entirely unanticipated by the Left.

## THE REAGAN EFFECT: LABOUR MISUNDERSTANDS AGAIN

To this day, the Left fails to acknowledge what those factors were. It was not Mikhail Gorbachev: it was largely Labour's *bête noire*, Ronald Reagan, though not quite for the reasons Reagan's conservative adulators believe.

Because of his ethical anti-Communism and commitment to a space-based ballistic missile defence (popularly termed 'Star Wars'), Reagan was seen – certainly by the British Left – as an uncomplicated warmonger. Yet Reagan was never the ideologue his critics (and some of his friends) assumed. He changed course radically on the issues of nuclear arms and US–Soviet relations at about the mid-point of his Presidency. Quite suddenly, in 1984, he adopted an altogether more pacific tone, and spent the rest of his term in office pursuing not only a more stable bilateral relationship but also a utopian vision of nuclear disarmament that matched the most fervent wishes of the peace campaigners who demonstrated against him.

Reagan's initial diplomatic turn at that juncture was correct and far-sighted, much as Kennedy's prudent management of the Cuban missile crisis had been. Yet his belief in worldwide nuclear disarmament was utterly misconceived. Reagan seems to have been strongly influenced by the Soviet response to the US and Nato military exercise in November 1983 known as 'Able Archer'. Oleg Gordievsky, then a British agent in the KGB, confirms that the Soviet leadership genuinely mistook this as evidence of a planned nuclear attack, to which their own military doctrine prescribed a pre-emptive nuclear strike. For reasons that remain unknown to Western analysts, they obviously did not follow that course. Almost from that moment, Reagan changed the emphasis of his diplomacy towards bilateral summitry and rhetorical reassurance, and took personal charge of foreign policy from his own State Department bureaucracy.[12]

This tells us much about Reagan that is at odds with the views of his detractors. First, he was prepared to adapt his statecraft to the world around him. Secondly, his biblical literalism and belief in Armageddon, so far from making him a 'trigger-happy' President, impressed upon him the urgency of preventing nuclear war. Thirdly, his personal direction of foreign policy refutes the notion of Reagan as a President dependent on his advisers. Fourthly, he put in place this change of policy *before* the appearance on the scene of *Time* magazine's badly-chosen 'Man of the Decade', Mikhail Gorbachev. Fifthly, the fact that the Soviet leadership so misconstrued Western intentions supports not the conventional peace movement case for détente and disarmament, but the liberal anti-Communist conviction – which Reagan articulated brilliantly – that pacific relations depend ultimately on the supersession of dictatorship rather than on negotiation with it.

Yet Reagan went a good deal further than these principles. As Henry Kissinger has pointed out:

> Reagan was impervious to much of the technical criticism [of his Strategic Defence Initiative] because he had not advocated SDI in strategic terms in the first place. Instead, he had presented it in terms of the 'liberal' cause of bringing about the abolition of nuclear war. The postwar president most committed to building up America's military strength, including its nuclear capacity, stood at the same time for a pacifist vision of a world from which all nuclear weapons were banished. Reagan's overused epigram that 'a nuclear war can never be won and must never be fought' was indistinguishable from the stated objectives of his radical critics.[13]

On the principle of a nuclear-free world, Reagan was wrong. As the recent failures of intelligence over Iraq's military capabilities have demonstrated, our knowledge of our adversaries is not good enough to allow confidence that genuine disarmament has taken place. A world in which nuclear weapons have supposedly been disinvented would in reality be a world in which nuclear weapons would be just about to be invented once more. In diplomatic crises, there would be a positive incentive for a protagonist to develop weapons rapidly and to launch them. Reagan's notions were wholly impractical and incidentally far outside mainstream politics in both the US and Great Britain.

There is a marvellous vignette illustrating this paradox by Kenneth Adelman, Reagan's director of the Arms Control and Disarmament Agency, in his memoir of that time, discussing the President's vision of complete nuclear disarmament:

> [My objections] never stuck at all with the President. He'd hear the arguments, respond to bits, and then reiterate his goal of a nuclear-free world. This vision was combined with a world of [SDI] defenses in a creative way, one only shared (to my knowledge) by fellow mystic, *New Yorker* writer Jonathan Schell. Indeed, in a New York discussion group once, I heard Schell spin out his utopian portrait later written in [his book] *Abolition*. I was dumbfounded and said that I had heard such notions from only one other person in my life, the President of the United States.[14]

A valuable influence here was Margaret Thatcher. As she records in *The Downing Street Years*, she felt 'as if there had been an earthquake beneath my feet' when Reagan attempted to act on this vision at the Reykjavik summit in 1986, thereby blunting the effectiveness of the West's nuclear deterrent. It was after her emergency trip to Camp David that that policy became more coherent and reputable. The President agreed to Mrs Thatcher's issuing a statement of support for an agreement with the Soviets on intermediate nuclear forces, a 50 per cent cut in strategic nuclear weapons over five years, the UK's acquisition of the Trident submarine programme and the continuation of SDI research. As regards the subsequent progress of the Cold War, the rest is history.

In short, Reagan, ever the butt of jokes about being simple and ill-informed, was a complex man with intellectual depths and subtle nuances to his politics. He contributed greatly to world peace and political liberty, because of his liberal principles *and* his willingness to calm the necessarily adversarial relationship with the Soviet Union at a crucial stage. Yet Reagan went beyond that record to a fanciful stance at odds with the policies of all American and West European governments since 1945. So far from being the natural ideological ally of Mrs Thatcher, he was, on this issue, her exact opposite.

The greatest irony of all from a British standpoint is that Labour, at the time committed to precisely that ideal of a world without nuclear weapons, was entirely unable to get the President's attention. In 1987 Kinnock and Healey visited the White House and were humiliated by Reagan's off-hand manner, in contrast to the public adulation that Mrs Thatcher was receiving at almost the same time on a visit to the Soviet Union. Healey recorded in his memoirs:

> When we entered the Oval Office, President Reagan
> strode immediately towards me, thrust out his hand,
> and said: 'Nice to meet you, Mr Ambassador!'
> The real Ambassador murmured plaintively:
> 'But I've already met him, *eleven* times.'[15]

It seems likely, contrary to Healey's inference, that Reagan was acting a part here, playing up to his image as (in the phrase of Clark Clifford) an amiable dunce. What he achieved by this apparent absent-mindedness and failure to master his brief was an unmistakable impression of his visitors' unimportance, by means other than an obviously intentional snub. It was a shame for Healey, but it was hardly an unfair comment on the international irrelevance that Labour had become. It is a mercy that irrelevance alone was its fate.

Two years later (and six years into his leadership), at a meeting of Labour's ruling National Executive to approve the party's Policy Review (8 and 9 May 1989), Kinnock belatedly arrived at a truism:

Many in this room have protested and marched in support
of nuclear disarmament. I have done something else:
I have gone to the White House, the Kremlin, the Elysee,
and argued the line for unilateral nuclear disarmament.
I knew they would disagree with the policy. But above
that, they were totally uncomprehending that we should
want to get rid of nuclear missile systems without getting
elimination of nuclear weapons on other sides too...
I am not going to make that tactical argument for that
unilateral abandonment of nuclear weapons without
getting anything in return. I will not do it. The majority
of the party and the majority of the country don't expect
me to do so.[16]

So ended – ingloriously and in language of purest pragma-
tism – Labour's association with the cause of unilateral nuclear
disarmament and the expulsion of US nuclear bases. It had
lasted considerably longer than an earlier flirtation with unilateralism, carried by a Labour conference vote in 1962 and
reversed by Labour leader Hugh Gaitskell and his supporters
the next year. The policy was a huge net vote loser that, coupled with poor (and in Foot's case, frivolous) leadership, had
brought Labour close to extinction as a serious political force
capable of challenging for government.

## THE PEACE MOVEMENT IN HISTORICAL PERSPECTIVE

Comparing the stance of British Labour at the origins of the
Cold War with its behaviour in the Second Cold War is bound
to be a different experience for a peace activist from that of a
liberal internationalist. Instead of a degeneration of a resolute
anti-totalitarianism, the peace activist will see a growing
awareness of the perils of nuclear diplomacy. Against those
dangers, ideological conflicts will be seen as of secondary
importance, or even trivial.

But the peace activist's view has been refuted by events as
much as anything can be. Contrary to the claims of CND, the
deployment of euromissiles (also known as INF, or intermediate nuclear forces) and the striving for a space-based ballistic

missile defence did not precipitate superpower tension. They forced the Soviet Union to the negotiating table, and eventually assisted its peaceful demise, to the immeasurable benefit of its subjects and everyone else. (On this point, we have the testimony of Aleksandr Bessmertnykh and Eduard Shevardnadze, who both served as Soviet Foreign Minister under Gorbachev: they are adamant that Reagan's Strategic Defence Initiative was crucial in convincing the Soviet Union that it had no alternative to concluding arms control agreements and undertaking internal reform.[17])

What was wrong in the Labour Party's stance in the 1980s is not quite the same question as what was wrong with the peace movement's. Labour professed loyalty to Nato throughout its anti-nuclear phase, with the result that its policy was scarcely coherent. Though there are non-nuclear members of Nato, Nato is a nuclear alliance. Proposing to expel the nuclear bases of Nato's leading participant was clearly not a loyal act, nor would it have been taken as such. CND, on the other hand, recognised the contradiction and campaigned explicitly for British withdrawal from Nato (a step that, were it ever to be accomplished in reality, would almost certainly be part of a Gaullist policy of nuclear-armed nationalism rather than a pacific stance).

But in posing unilateral nuclear disarmament as the centrepiece of foreign policy, Labour and the peace movement were as one. In much of the public debate about nuclear disarmament and relations with the Soviet Union in the 1980s, this position was denounced as appeasement, but this was not strictly right. A more accurate comparison is with the professed believers in collective security in the 1930s who refused to accept that there were greater evils than rearmament.

What the modern disarmers failed to understand was that the enemy was not nuclear weapons, but the political relations between states of which those weapons were a symbol. The struggle for peace was indivisible from the struggle for human rights. Almost by its nature, the disarmament movement failed to give sufficient weight to the moral and strategic requirements of undermining totalitarianism through containment and elements of 'rollback'. This is a failure of political judgement that carries through to the more recent debates about the promotion of global democracy as a means of defeating Islamist totalitarianism.

But one last observation should be made about the peace campaigns of the 1980s. In the 1930s some genuine idealists of the Left supported the peace movement, and many of these came to understand that campaigning simultaneously against fascism and war was an impossible position. Totalitarianism was not the sort of enemy that allowed for peaceful relations except on its own terms and under its own domination: peace meant, and could only mean, a *Pax Germanica*. Moreover, even those who persisted in their illusions (George Orwell for one) almost until, or after, war was declared, did so not necessarily out of any equivocation regarding the evils of fascism. But there was, as we have seen, a disturbing undercurrent of romanticism regarding totalitarianism. Some of this was moral frivolity; some of it was sinister.

In the early stages of the Cold War, the British Left, dominated by the Labour Party (which was also the most successful of European democratic parties of the Left), absorbed and learned from these errors, on seeing the aggressive designs of Soviet Communism. The cause of an independent – or even a pro-Soviet - foreign policy did have influential supporters who proved durable, but they were very much a minority, especially after the coup in Czechoslovakia. In the Second Cold War, however, the make-up of the disarmament campaign proved reminiscent of trends in the 1930s. A more benign view of Communist totalitarianism – stressing its supposed social advances and its pacific intent – permeated anti-nuclear propaganda, even from people who were not themselves Communists. It is difficult to find any natural limits to the credulity of some Labour MPs at this time. One of them, Stan Newens, wrote copiously in the 1970s of the progressive example set by the Romanian tyrant Nicolae Ceausescu, who apparently presented:

an overwhelming case for Britain to adopt an independent
foreign policy. This would...bring us closer to countries
like Rumania and would accelerate the development of
the demand for the withdrawal of troops on both sides
and ultimately the winding up of both military blocs.[18]

Newens was surely sincere in his beliefs, but as it happens
new historical information has emerged in the past decade –
principally from the archives of the East German secret police,
the Stasi – that sheds light on the process whereby peace campaigners became credulous conduits for messages of the peace-
able character of Communism. The peace movement was not
itself a conscious arm of Stasi or Soviet intelligence, but it is
beyond question that hostile powers saw peace campaigners as
a rich potential source of sympathisers and active agents.[19] The
name of one of them entered the public domain in 1999.
A former member of CND's National Council, Professor
Vic Allen, told the BBC that he had been a Stasi spy. CND's
response to the news was revealing. Its chairman, Dave Knight,
stated in a press release dated 19 September 1999:

> We all knew where Vic stood – he was entitled to his views
> and we were entitled to ours. He most certainly did not
> 'swing CND behind the Soviets' and nor did anyone else.
> CND was and remains independent of all governments
> and neither the Stasi, the KGB, the CIA nor our own MI5
> have [sic] ever managed to change that.

So by its own account – and recall that this press release is
intended as its *defence* – CND had known that its National
Council contained at least one vocal advocate for totalitarianism, yet it regarded this affiliation as merely a personal idiosyncrasy: one view among many within the movement.

Those who tried in the 1980s to get the Labour Party to
abandon nuclear pacifism and return to its traditional commitment to the Atlantic alliance occasionally wondered about the
role of foreign intelligence services in the often inflammatory
propaganda of the peace movement. (Such propaganda, for

example, would typically allege that Cruise missiles deployed in Europe were 'first-strike' weapons, suggesting that they were intended for aggressive purposes rather than deterrence.) We now know for a fact that the boundary separating legitimate anti-nuclear campaigning from deliberate anti-Western subversion was porous and badly policed. By regarding support for tyranny as a personal idiosyncrasy rather than anything more culpable, CND demonstrated its own untrustworthiness in policy debate.

1 Clement Attlee, *The Labour Party in Perspective* (London: Victor Gollancz, 1937), p. 226.

2 *Ibid.* p. 227.

3 Kenneth O. Morgan, *Labour in Power, 1945–51* (Oxford: Oxford University Press, 1984), p. 262.

4 Quoted in Kenneth Harris, *Attlee* (London: Weidenfeld and Nicolson, 1982), p. 288.

5 Lena Jeger, Obituary for John Platts-Mills, *Guardian*, 27 October 2001.

6 Archie Potts, *Zilliacus: A Life for Peace and Socialism* (London: Merlin Press, 2002).

7 George Orwell, 'In defence of Comrade Zilliacus', in *The Collected Essays, Journalism and Letters of George Orwell*, ed. Ian Angus and Sonia Orwell (London: Penguin, 1968), Volume 4, p. 453.

8 Potts, *Zilliacus*, p. 112.

9 *Ibid.* p. 96; Potts includes Attlee's matchless reply: 'Thank you for sending me your memorandum which seems to me to be based on an astonishing lack of understanding of the facts.'

10 R. Palme Dutt, *Mr Bevin's Record*, published under the auspices of the Communist journal *Labour Monthly*, n.d. but clearly from 1949–50. A minor indication of the temper of the times on the Left came at a debate between Dutt and A. J. P. Taylor at the Oxford University Labour Club in June 1949. Dutt's biographer records, 'The audience greeted him with loud, derisive laughter after he told them that Communists were not afraid to admit their mistakes' (John Callaghan, *Rajani Palme Dutt: A Study in British Stalinism* [London: Lawrence and Wishart, 1993], p. 234).

11 Quoted in Peter Jones, *America and the British Labour Party* (London: Tauris Academic Studies, 1997), pp. 192–3.

12 The evidence is presented in compelling fashion by Beth A. Fischer, *The Reagan Reversal* (Columbia: University of Missouri Press, 2000).

13 Henry Kissinger, *Diplomacy* (New York: Simon and Schuster, 1994), pp. 780–1.

14 Kenneth Adelman, The *Great Universal Embrace* (New York: Simon and Schuster, 1989), p. 68.

15 Denis Healey, *The Time of My Life* (London: Michael Joseph, 1989), p. 534.

16 Cited in C. Hughes and P. Wintour, *Labour Rebuilt: The New Model Party* (London: Fourth Estate, 1990), p. 107.

17 Both are cited in Andrew Busch, *Ronald Reagan and the Politics of Freedom* (New York: Rowan and Littlefield, 2001), p. 201.

18 *Nicolae Ceausescu: a selection from his speeches and writings*, introduction by Stan Newens (1973), cited in Darren G. Lilleker, *Against the Cold War: The History and Political Traditions of Pro-Sovietism in the British Labour Party, 1945–89* (London: Tauris Academic Studies, 2004), p. 144.

19 On this, for the British case, see Anthony Glees, *The Stasi Files* (London: Free Press, 2003), especially Chapter 12. In the US too, while you might have thought it would be a rational strategy to recruit only those who were clandestine rather than active sympathisers, the Stasi recruited agents who made no secret of their political sympathies.
In 1997 an FBI sting caught three American former Stasi agents, Theresa Squillacote, her husband Kurt Stand and James Michael Clark, after they had – with astonishing ineptitude – volunteered their services to someone they mistakenly thought was a South African Communist. All had been active in Communist organisations since the 1970s; despite her profession as a Pentagon lawyer, Squillacote was an open member of the pro-Soviet Committees of Correspondence up until, and indeed after, her arrest.

CHAPTER 3

REGIME CHANGE

*I think Iraq will be remarkable. We're going to live
to see great things. We already have in Lebanon.
We're about to, I think, in Egypt, with the reopening
of the Egyptian democracy. The Baath party in Syria,
in my judgement, will not be there in two years' time.
And there will be extraordinary, are already extraordinary,
developments in Iran, which I have just come back from.
And so the essential point of the Blair–Bush policy,
which is to change the balance of power in the Middle
East – that has already been conclusively vindicated.*
Christopher Hitchens, BBC Radio 4, *Start the Week*, 30 May 2005

## 'AUTUMN OF THE AUTOCRATS'

Quite suddenly, in the spring of 2005, demand for political
reform coalesced in a part of the world so far resistant to constitutional democracy.

Despite intimidation and murderous incursions by groups
inaptly dignified by media commentators with the term
'insurgents', nine million Iraqis voted in the country's first
post-Baathist election in January 2005. Protests in Lebanon
led to the withdrawal of Syrian troops after a 29-year occupation. Elections in May registered a decisive rejection of Syrian
influence. Saudi Arabia conceded municipal elections (though
with an all-male franchise). Egypt laid plans for competitive
presidential elections. Syria's Baathist regime felt the diplomatic
pressure of change in Lebanon so keenly that its youthful
autocrat, Bashar al-Assad, immediately – and fruitlessly –
sought fraternal support from Saudi Arabia. A state that has
supported and given sanctuary to various terrorist causes and
operatives for 30 years is increasingly diplomatically isolated
in the region, save for another longstanding state-sponsor of
terrorism, Iran.

Meanwhile the death of Yassir Arafat precipitated a warming of relations between the Palestinians and Israel, assisted by elections in the Palestinian Authority. The prospects for a negotiated territorial accommodation between Israel and the Palestinians, with a supposedly obdurate and hawkish Israeli Prime Minister at the helm, suddenly looked brighter than at any time since the Oslo Accord. Tony Blair was guardedly hopeful. In a newspaper interview he declared:

> There is a genuine ripple of change at the moment but it is happening throughout the Middle East and it is important that we encourage it because it is out of [the Middle East] that so many of the issues that we grapple with in the international community arise.[1]

Blair was reticent on the sequence of events. An unusually candid *Guardian* columnist acknowledged, however, that if Blair 'had wanted to brag and claim credit – boasting that the toppling of Saddam Hussein had set off a benign chain reaction – he would have had plenty of evidence to call on'.[2] The London-based International Institute for Strategic Studies, often sceptical of US administration policy and wary of what it identified as 'the inspirational effect of the Iraq intervention on transnational Islamist terrorism', also concluded: 'On balance, U.S. policy in 2004–2005 appeared fairly effective in emboldening regional actors in the Middle East and Gulf to rally against rogue states and implement gentle political reforms.'[3]

Syria became a particular focus after the assassination of former Lebanese Prime Minister Rafiq Hariri in February 2005, as Bush insisted on the removal of Syrian troops from Lebanon. These developments were not yet an Arab Spring; the Middle East scholar Fouad Ajami, of Johns Hopkins University, raised the prospect that they might mark the 'autumn of the autocrats'. He noted:

There was no small irony in this twist of history: fifteen years earlier, George H. W. Bush and Hafiz al-Assad had struck a deal that liquidated Lebanon's independence; now their sons were bringing that deal to an end. It was fitting that the edifice of Syrian control secured in the first campaign against Saddam was being undone in the course of the second.[4]

## THE IMPORTANCE OF REGIME CHANGE

This recent experience is worth rehearsing, because it goes some way to validating the grand strategy pursued by the US with the support of the UK since 9/11. Critics of the Bush/Blair approach dispute this, maintaining that citing Arab reforms as a consequence of regime change in Afghanistan and Iraq is a *post hoc ergo propter hoc* fallacy. The stirrings of political liberty are subsequent to, but not consequent upon, the Bush doctrine of promoting global democracy.

But the critics are evasive. The reason for attributing to the Bush Administration and Blair Government primary responsibility for the shake-up in the politics of the Middle East is that that was the announced aim of policy in the first place. It was the plan, and if it is premature to say that the plan is working, then at least the plan is consequential. In his State of the Union address on 2 February 2005, President Bush stated:

> To promote peace and stability in the broader Middle East, the United States will work with our friends in the region to fight the common threat of terror, while we encourage a higher standard of freedom...To promote peace in the broader Middle East, we must confront regimes that continue to harbor terrorists and pursue weapons of mass murder. Syria still allows its territory, and parts of Lebanon, to be used by terrorists who seek to destroy every chance of peace in the region. You have passed, and we are applying, the Syrian Accountability Act – and we expect the Syrian government to end all support for terror and open the door to freedom.[5]

The crux of the case for the Bush/Blair approach is the link between Western security and political institutions. Blair immediately saw the issue for what it was, because it was one he had applied earlier in his premiership. In the months preceding the Iraq War it was thought politic – though was clearly in the longer run damaging – to stress what turned out to be bad intelligence on Saddam's arsenal, but there was always a more fundamental reason for promoting international regime change. It was reactive strategy, in the sense that it responded to the patent vulnerability of Western societies to Islamist terrorism; it was also anticipatory, in that it aimed to remove the conditions that bred such fanaticism.

## TERRORISM AND ITS CAUSES

The notion of the 'root causes' of terrorism rapidly became a cliché after 9/11. Whenever these root causes were enumerated, they turned out to be whatever the critic concerned had been campaigning about on and before 9/10 – among many others, world poverty, a Palestinian state, or global warming. A representative example comes from the then President of the Methodist Conference, Rev. Neil Richardson, speaking immediately after the Madrid bombings in March 2004:

> The perpetrators of the Madrid bombings, and their particular motivations, have not yet been identified. But what is incontestable is that global terrorism, of which Spain is the most recent victim, is bred by injustice and deprivation. Western nations, therefore, need critically to examine their foreign policy.[6]

As we shall see, Mr Richardson's assertion is not 'incontestable' at all. It is a speculative hypothesis at odds with the conclusions of empirical research.

For some reason, liberal Protestant clergymen seem particularly susceptible to invoking root causes, but sober and well-informed commentators on public policy show the same inclination. Again among many other examples, a recent book by a highly experienced financial columnist, John Plender of the *Financial Times*, stands out. Plender presents a thoughtful case against systemic failings in the Anglo-American model of global capitalism. Suddenly, amid an impressive marshalling of evidence and economic reasoning about the political constraints on US monetary policy in deflating asset price bubbles and the vulnerability of well-managed developing-country economies to shifts in short-term capital flows, Plender comes out with this:

> He [an African economist of Plender's acquaintance] retired prematurely to spend more time in Senegal where he immersed himself in Sufism, the Islamic form of mysticism. It was a similar protest, but in a civilised and humane form, to that of the Islamic terrorists who wrecked the twin towers in New York – a profound expression of impotence, marginalisation and despair.[7]

Plender, one-time recipient of the Wincott Prize for Financial Journalism and Chairman of the Advisory Council of the Centre for the Study of Financial Innovation, has spent his professional life discussing technical subjects with reasonable people. Because he cannot credit that some people are driven by atavistic impulses, he naturally assumes that the rhetorical – never mind actual – violence of Islamist terror must be code for something else.

Least surprising in any survey of opinion on the causes of terrorism is the resistance of the ostensibly Marxist Left to re-examining its presumptions about the sources of oppression in the modern world. The late Paul Foot wrote in his *Guardian* column a month after 9/11:

> Appeasement of Israel has been the lynchpin of US and British policy in the Middle East, and is obviously connected, at whatever distance, to the terrorist attacks on September 11.[8]

'At whatever distance' is a useful formulation in these debates because it is impervious to being falsified. Whatever distance you travel, you can always travel further and thereby maintain that the connection exists even if it has not yet been uncovered (many of the White House's assertions of the links between Saddam Hussein and al-Qaeda have had this quality). Of course there is some connection between Western policy on Israel and al-Qaeda's murderous ideology, because Israel is a Jewish state and al-Qaeda urges holy war on Jews. There is nothing Israel can do to meet al-Qaeda's minimal requirements, because the minimal requirement is death. That is the point: al-Qaeda's programme is not a set of negotiable grievances but an apocalyptic pursuit of the annihilation of Western civilisation.

That is not merely what al-Qaeda is accused of: it is what al-Qaeda says. As the author of the first and best book to have been published about Osama bin Laden after 9/11 has explained:

> Bin Laden articulates an all-encompassing world view with a much wider appeal than simple hatred of Israel. Of course, he is opposed to Israel, but he also calls for the end of US military actions against Iraq; demands the creation of a 'Muslim' nuclear weapon; claims it is a religious obligation to attack American military and civilian targets worldwide because of the continued presence of US troops in the Gulf; criticises the governments of countries like Egypt and Saudi Arabia for not instituting what he sees as true Islamic law; and supports a multitude of holy wars around the globe.[9]

The premises of this all-encompassing world view are less Delphic than Western columnists suppose. The ideology of Islamist totalitarianism is neither subtle nor despairing: it is an assertion of theocratic triumphalism over the values of the Enlightenment. In a statement dated 23 February 1998, under the auspices of the 'International Islamic Front for Jihad on the Jews and Crusaders', Osama bin Laden urged:

The ruling to kill the Americans and their allies –
civilians and military – is an individual duty for every
Muslim who can do it in any country in which it is
possible to do it, in order to liberate the al-Aqsa mosque
and the holy mosque [Mecca] from their grip, and in
order for their armies to move out of all the lands of
Islam, defeated and unable to threaten any Muslim...
We – with God's help – call on every Muslim who
believes in God and wishes to be rewarded to comply
with God's order to kill the Americans and plunder
their money wherever and whenever they find it.[10]

In an interview broadcast on al-Jazeera television, December 1998, bin Laden expounded uncomplicatedly the premise of his terrorism:

Every Muslim, the minute he can start differentiating,
carries hate toward Americans, Jews, and Christians:
this is part of our ideology. Ever since I can recall I felt
at war with the Americans and had feelings of animosity
and hate toward them.[11]

The standard radical critique of American assertiveness ends up embodying the ethnocentrism it professes to transcend. Intent on ascribing its own disaffection to militant Islam, it fails to grasp the latter's ideological character. When bin Laden asserts (in his 1998 statement 'The Nuclear Bomb of Islam') that 'it is the duty of Muslims to prepare as much force as possible to terrorize the enemies of God', he is not calling for looser conditionality in the implementation of IMF structural adjustment programmes. When Paul Foot writes, after listing half a dozen of his own complaints about the international order (including the misogyny of Saudi society, the eradication of which has unaccountably not featured among the Jihadists' demands), 'That doesn't excuse the fanatical and suicidal terrorism of September 11 but it helps to explain it', he states not only a dubious political thesis but also a factual error. Foot's catechism does not begin to explain Islamist terrorism, because it does not examine critically what the Islamists stand for. It is a conceptual as well as a moral evasion. As the *New York Times* columnist Thomas Friedman has observed,

> One can only be amazed at the ease with which some people abroad and at campus teach-ins now tell us what motivated the terrorists. Guess what? The terrorists didn't leave an explanatory note. Because their deed was their note: We want to destroy America, starting with its military and financial centers. Which part of that sentence don't people understand?[12]

Issues of poverty, inequality, women's rights and social reforms are important in themselves, but they are germane to the struggle against Islamist totalitarianism only in the sense that it is the best features of Western liberal societies and not the worst that inflame our enemies. There is literally nothing that the US and her allies can do about the social injustices that we tolerate or even contribute to that would dissuade those who are bent on the destruction of Western civilisation and its replacement by a restored Caliphate. The only possible response to theocratic totalitarianism from the adherents and defenders of Western civilisation – those of diverse views on other matters but who value in common the Enlightenment principles of free inquiry, separation of civil and religious authority, liberal political rights, the pursuit of science and reason, sexual equality, pluralism and tolerance – is militant opposition.

But there is a sense in which it is right and important to talk of root causes. Recent academic research suggests that the 'root cause' of terrorism is not poverty – if it were then sub-Saharan Africa would be the obvious source of anti-Western terror – but political repression. Societies where dissent is confined to religious absolutism are incubators of violent anti-Western fanaticism. The authors of one study, the Princeton economist Alan B. Krueger and Jitka Maleckova of Charles University in Prague, found that apart from size of population – more populated countries tend to have more terrorists – the only variable consistently associated with the incidence of terrorism was the Freedom House index of political liberties and civil rights: 'Countries with more freedom were less likely to be the birthplace of international terrorists. Poverty and literacy were unrelated to the number of terrorists from a country...' They hypothesised that terrorism, rather than being generated by poverty or lack of education, is 'more accurately viewed as a response to political conditions and longstanding feelings of indignity and frustration that have little to do with economic circumstances'.[13]

The case for overthrowing despotism in Iraq could be, and ought to have been, stated in a way at least as succinct as the claims of Saddam's WMDs and with much greater plausibility. Without a decisive intervention to remove the worst of governments and assist the Iraqi people to build a constitutional democracy, the pathologies tolerated by autocratic regimes would burgeon.

## COUNTER-TERRORIST STRATEGIES

Before discussing the case for overthrowing Saddam Hussein specifically, we should consider one conundrum about the defeat of terrorism. Many commentators have expended unnecessary ingenuity in interpreting the aims of Islamist terrorists, when those aims are not obscure at all. They are open, apocalyptic and acted-upon. But even though the ideological objectives are non-negotiable, the transitional demands may be carefully constructed to exert political pressure.

This question has been raised in discussions of the work of a Chicago academic, Robert Pape. In an article published in 2003,[14] Pape drew inferences from his database of every recorded instance of suicide terrorism (comprising 188 attacks, in countries including Lebanon, Sri Lanka, India and Turkey, and in the West Bank) between 1980 and 2001. He has updated his work to 2003 (comprising 315 attacks) in a recent book.[15]

Pape disputes the identification of suicide terrorism with Islamist militancy, observing that the principal instigator of suicide terrorism is the Tamil Tiger movement in Sri Lanka (responsible for 76 of the acts recorded by Pape), a secular group. He maintains that suicide bombings are almost invariably part of a wider political or military campaign, that democracies in particular are vulnerable to the tactic, and that this form of terrorism is employed to advance a strategic end, such as national self-determination or the expulsion of US forces from the Arabian Gulf. In the context of al-Qaeda he argues that suicide terrorism is primarily a response to foreign occupation, rather than a function of religious fanaticism, and he cautions that a strategy of trying to spread democracy in the Middle East is liable to generate rather than dampen suicide terrorism.

Pape's work has been criticised by other researchers on three main grounds. First, there are concerns about the quality of his data. Pape's 'universe' of suicide-terrorist attacks is not a universe, as it contains only around half of the total,[16] while many attacks appear to have been wrongly described or classified. Martin Kramer, of Tel Aviv University, complains that 'reading through Pape's database of suicide attacks for the place and period I know best – Lebanon in the mid-1980s – I kept encountering operations that I couldn't remember at all, or that I remembered as having different authors than the ones he names, or that I remembered as having killed far fewer people than appear in his "killed" column'.[17]

Secondly, Pape understates the pathological character of Islamist terrorism. Daniel Benjamin of the Center for Strategic and International Studies, formerly an official in the Clinton Administration working on counterterrorism, is wary of identifying too precise a strategic rationale of al-Qaeda's terrorism: 'To try to reduce it to an agenda that is purely political is to misunderstand religion. The reason that bin Laden and his followers want the U.S. out of the Middle East has religious roots.' Moreover, it is accurate to see suicide terrorism as a predominantly Islamist threat so far as it relates to the security needs of Western powers. According to Bruce Hoffman, a specialist in counterterrorism and counterinsurgency at the RAND Corporation, 31 out of 35 groups employing suicide terrorism are Islamist in inspiration.[18]

As it turned out, Pape's work was published in book-length form only a matter of weeks before suicide bombers killed more than 50 people in London on 7 July 2005. The bombings dealt a blow to Pape's thesis that this form of terrorism is a response to foreign occupation, rather than an expression of religious fanaticism. Even allowing for the broadest possible interpretation of 'foreign occupation' to include the objection of young Western Islamists to the occupation of Iraq, we are still left with an inadequate account of the motivations of terrorists. One of the London bombers, Germaine Lindsay, was of Jamaican origin and had never even visited Iraq, yet he bade his pregnant wife and child goodbye before blowing himself up, along with 26 commuters, at King's Cross. 'Politics', or even 'ideology', scarcely offers the explanation his widow pitifully sought in observing that she had 'never predicted or imagined that he was involved in such horrific activities'.[19] Even 'religious fanaticism' is too weak a term for this destructive nihilism.

The third problem with Pape's work is that his policy conclusions are highly disputable on the basis of his own analysis. His work points to an important characteristic of suicide missions. Suicide bombing does not fit a pattern of random destruction and is not born of despair. It is a political tactic that may, on occasion, gain advantages for the perpetrator. Examples that Pape cites are the evacuation of American and French forces from Lebanon in 1983, the Sri Lankan government's granting Tamil independence from 1990, and the Turkish government's granting Kurdish autonomy in the late 1990s. Pape concludes:

> This pattern of making concessions to suicide terrorist organizations over the past two decades has probably encouraged terrorist groups to pursue even more ambitious suicide campaigns.

In short, suicide terrorism is a calculated act in furtherance of political ends. In the case of al-Qaeda, its equivalents and its surrogates, those ends are millenarian and unrealisable, but the movement still advances transitional demands as a stage towards achieving its maximalist ends. Though the Madrid bombings in 2004 were not suicide bombings (the ten bombs were detonated remotely by using the alarm function on cell phones), they conformed to this pattern. Plainly designed to affect an electoral outcome, they helped secure the withdrawal of Spanish troops from Iraq.

This much is true and even standard reasoning about this type of terrorism. But, as Martin Kramer observes:

> Pape does a last-minute twist, arguing that the most effective response would be an American disengagement from the Middle East and Israeli withdrawal from the Palestinian territories. The United States and Israel should stand back and hunker down behind defensive perimeters. Why? This would diminish the incentives (read: grievances) behind strategic suicide bombing. I find this conclusion completely at odds with the analysis. Wouldn't this be the ultimate concession to the suicide strategy – and be celebrated as such by its planners? Wouldn't this inspire yet more mutations of the method, and the expansion of the terrorists' strategic goals?[20]

If the answers to Kramer's questions are 'yes' – as I believe they are – then frustrating those intermediate goals is an integral part of defeating Islamist totalitarianism. Grand strategy must be supported by political tactics. This matters. While many commentators mistake the character of terrorism as a cry of despair rather than an act of war, few are so uncomprehending as to suppose that Islamist terrorists can be directly negotiated with in an attempt to propitiate their complaints.[21] But the principle of adopting a non-threatening and non-provocative posture towards terrorists is a tenacious one, as is the notion that a negotiated resolution of violent conflict will dispel the conditions in which terrorism thrives.

These hopes are bound to be disappointed, and if acted upon they are liable to damage the capacity of Western civilisation to defend itself. Granted that the foreign policies of Western nations generate hatred that in turn stimulates terrorism – and I see little purpose in denying it in order to present a sanitised assessment of the consequences of an interventionist foreign policy – it is almost impossible to conceive of a foreign policy we could pursue that would not have that outcome. Consider again bin Laden's 1998 call for Muslims to liberate 'the holy mosque from [America's] grip', i.e. to expel American troops from Saudi Arabia. The troops were there to deter an attack by Saddam Hussein on his neighbours. Saddam needed to be deterred because Coalition forces had deliberately left him in power at the end of the Gulf War, in accord with the letter of UN Security Council resolutions authorising force only to expel him from Kuwait. The departure of almost all US troops was conditional on, and has followed from, Saddam's removal from power.

Had Saddam been left in power and US and British forces been withdrawn from the region, the consequences would have been disastrous. It would have been disastrous for the Kurds of Northern Iraq, protected by the no-fly zones patrolled for years previously by British and American pilots; for the sovereignty of Kuwait, which in 1990 had been plundered, annexed and made into the 19th province of Iraq; for the Shi'ah Muslims of Southern Iraq; for Saudi Arabia and Israel; and, not least, for the advanced industrial economies, faced with a newly powerful oil-producing nation. Had Saddam been left in power but with US and British troops stationed in the region to protect those he threatened, the Islamist fury would have been in no wise abated. If Saddam's overthrow (which has allowed the US to withdraw troops from Saudi Arabia) has generated terrorism against us, then leaving him in power (requiring the continued deployment of those troops) would have had the same outcome, *as would any other course we might have taken.*

As a rule, there is no purpose in gratuitous provocation in foreign policy, but the provocation offered to Islamist extremism is inevitable whatever we do, and something of which we should be proud. Why deny that the West's role in allowing an independent Timor (which bin Laden counts as part of the Islamic world) to emerge from Indonesian tutelage has inflamed Islamist terror?[22] Or that our enemies are incensed by our promotion of women's emancipation and legal rights for homosexuals?

Even a purely isolationist policy such as that favoured by obscurantist conservatives such as Pat Buchanan or the Little Englander tendency in British politics (on the Left as much as the anti-European and anti-American Right) would provide no escape. The negligence and amorality of European governments in failing to counter Serb aggression against Bosnia in the early 1990s were not lost on bin Laden, who took this episode as one further instance of the West's criminal and bellicose anti-Muslim policies.[23] Whatever we do, or fail to do, we will be a target, and so will others for whom – if liberal or socialist internationalism is to mean anything – we have a responsibility. We might as well, therefore, do the right thing.

The prospect of negotiating settlements to other violent conflicts with terrorist movements – IRA, ETA, FARC, arguably Hamas – that pursue less absolutist goals than al-Qaeda is popular and more plausible, even in the case of terrorist groups that use suicide bombings.[24] It is still wrong. True, some terrorist groups may eventually be weaned on to constitutional politics, just as the old Official IRA eventually metamorphosed into the Workers' Party. But a democratic polity cannot know in advance which groups fall into which category. The most reliable way to find out is to force the choice upon them by treating them without differentiation as if they are all inveterate and enduring enemies of civilisation.

This approach turns on its head the philosophy of matching a suspension of terrorist violence with political concessions; it offers no concessions at all. Its rationale is to convince terrorists that their goals are unattainable and thus that their alternatives are to sue for peace or face extirpation. Its message is not 'extend your ceasefire', but 'abandon violence irrevocably or we will hit you again and again, not to contain you but to destroy you'. It is, for example, a myth that IRA terrorism proved impervious to such an approach. A former Labour Northern Ireland Secretary, Roy Mason, came to office in 1976 eschewing political initiatives and promising to roll up the IRA 'like a tube of toothpaste'. His efforts had a discernible effect on the IRA's operational effectiveness and precipitated a drastic reduction in terrorist activity. An earlier IRA campaign, begun in 1957, was repelled by the Irish government by internment, among other indelicate means. Conor Cruise O'Brien, a Cabinet minister in the 1970s, later reflected, 'I am convinced that if the later IRA offensive, begun in 1971, had been met with the same determination in the Republic, it too could have been brought to an early end.'[25]

Similarly, Israel's much-criticised policy of targeted assassinations directed against successive leaders of Hamas is part of a pragmatic policy of inflicting heavy costs on terrorist groups. That approach caused Hizbollah to reassess its use of suicide bombing, a technique it had initiated in the early 1980s, on a straightforward assessment that it was not working. Attacking Hamas directly while withdrawing unilaterally from the Gaza settlements could hardly be bettered as a pacific policy: it demonstrates seriousness about territorial accommodation, while discharging the Palestinian Authority's own treaty obligations – never observed – to crack down on terrorism. The approach that Western governments should adopt indiscriminately in the case of terrorist organisations is to acknowledge that diplomacy has a limit, quite as much as does force. If diplomacy has no limit then terrorists will understand it as an opportunity to gain political advantage by continuing with violence. That would have been the arrangement had Coalition forces not overthrown the Taliban in Afghanistan as an initial stage in the campaign of regime change.

This is a general principle, but even those who conceive of exceptions to it would have difficulty identifying them in the case of al-Qaeda, sheltered by the Taliban. It is worth recalling that the anti-war movement argued after 9/11 that we should test the Taliban's good faith by demanding bin Laden's extradition, and that a bombing campaign would catastrophically disrupt aid programmes. The most extreme of its partisans managed to construe the US as a genocidal power. Noam Chomsky depicted mass starvation as a conscious choice of US policy, declaring that 'plans are being made and programmes implemented on the assumption that they may lead to the death of several million people in the next couple of weeks... very casually, with no comment, no particular thought about it, that's just kind of normal, here, and in a good part of Europe.'[26]

Chomsky's judgement was offered without evidence and in apparent wilful ignorance of the US's documented support for the relief efforts of UN agencies. Diplomacy was of no use in dealing with the terrorists sheltered by the Taliban in Afghanistan. The bombing campaign greatly assisted the delivery of aid to Afghanistan by removing from power the people who for years had been expropriating it. Since the Taliban's fall, more than 3.5 million refugees have chosen to return to Afghanistan, anticipating a better life for themselves.[27] Whatever its teething pains, Afghanistan is an emerging constitutional democracy that has replaced a theocratic tyranny that, among other things, banned kites and murdered homosexuals by toppling walls on to them.

In serving Afghanistan by the humanitarian act of overthrowing a mediaeval barbarism and thereby removing the principal constraint on humanitarian assistance, the US and its allies also served their own security needs. As well as overthrowing the Taliban, they cornered an organisation responsible for the murder of thousands of civilians, killed the terrorist leader who had planned the bombings of the US embassies in Tanzania and Kenya in 1998, and protected American lives by demonstrating to potential aggressors a willingness to defend themselves. They also protected Afghan lives. Even the most extreme estimate of the civilian deaths attributable to the bombing campaign – a politicised and incompetent survey which came to a figure of around 4,000[28] – would roughly match a single atrocity carried out by the Taliban in August 1998, when it massacred thousands of Shi'ah Hazaras.

The case of Afghanistan also raised the question of sovereignty, and showed how problematic that concept is when countries are taken over by an illegitimate regime. The intervention to overthrow the Taliban was humanitarian not only in the sense that it removed an appalling set of rulers: it was also, strictly speaking, a national liberation struggle. The nominal host country was, in effect, run by a transplanted Islamist group, generally recruited from Arab states. This was what made the peace movement's demand for diplomacy to secure the extradition of bin Laden surreal.[29] The symbiosis between al-Qaeda and the Taliban was not a normal relationship between a host government and a non-state actor. The Taliban could no more hand over bin Laden than it could Lord Lucan.

The overthrow of the Taliban was a just war and a necessary initial task. But an initial task is what it was.

## WHY SADDAM?

To say the Bush Administration has made innumerable errors in its conduct of war and occupation is commonplace but not trivial: it is true and important. But the first error, from which much else has flowed, was to plan for occupation after Saddam's fall in a fundamentally non-serious manner. Elections were delayed; security was inadequate; the failure to secure Baghdad was a disaster; infrastructure was ignored; abominable tortures were practised at the Abu Ghraib prison, to which there was a shamefully complacent response; and the civilian death toll appears to have been substantially higher than the war's supporters generally expected.[30] These deficiencies and crimes were compounded because we had no idea to what extent civil society in Iraq had ceased to exist under Saddam. That is not an argument against regime change: it is a rueful historical reflection that our intervention came too late, but nonetheless did good. Had we allowed the regime to persist, the consequences for the people of Iraq of an Uday–Qusay dynasty would have been desperate. Had the regime eventually imploded under – as it were – the weight of its own contradictions, it would have become the happy-hunting ground of Islamist terrorists throughout the region. The line between a rogue state and a failed state is, as we would have found, a thin one. The notion that terrorism has been brought to Iraq uniquely by the West's overthrow of Saddam is myopic.

Despite its culpable failings in the occupation of Iraq, the Bush Administration has one continuing strength in its approach to security: it has a more synoptic view of the struggle against terror than have its political opponents. A common refrain in the arguments over the Iraq War was that it was a diversion from the pursuit of those responsible for 9/11. This was a notable feature of the Democrat campaign for the White House, with Senator John Kerry maintaining fruitlessly: 'The invasion of Iraq was a profound diversion from the battle against our greatest enemy – al Qaeda...George Bush made Saddam Hussein the priority. I would have made Osama bin Laden the priority.' So far as any consistent theme in Michael Moore's mendacious film *Fahrenheit 9/11* could be discerned, the message was similar. But it was wrong.

The anti-war movement implicitly saw the attack on the Twin Towers as a discrete event to be countered by means of better law-enforcement, police work and diplomatic pressure. This was a sincere view (at least among those not allied to the movement's totalitarian wing) but one that lacked a sense of the gravity of the threat. Some of its proponents lacked also a sense of the ridiculous. The septuagenarian anti-nuclear campaigner Bruce Kent told *The New Statesman*: 'I think we need to pursue Bin Laden in different ways: for example, by blocking communications to Afghanistan. I would even go as far as combing through bank accounts across the world and freezing anything suspicious.' In these dark times, the erstwhile Monsignor would *even open a bank statement that was not addressed to him*. An exclusively juridical approach to fighting terror would founder on the brute fact that international law lacks a sovereign body capable of implementing it, other than the states that subscribe to it. More prosaically, what would happen if bin Laden failed to respond to a court summons is not a scenario generally discussed in the literature of the peace movement (and I have tried to find it).

But beyond the organised anti-war movement, the Iraq sceptics – those who doubted the grand strategy of the Bush Administration and the support given it by Tony Blair – made a comparable, if not directly equivalent, oversight. It assumed that, because the evidence of direct links between al-Qaeda and Saddam Hussein was weak, the wars against both were separate. The Bush Administration did its own case much harm in this debate, by overstressing what evidence did exist and positing an 'axis of evil' among states that, while unquestionably all evil, were nonetheless sufficiently heterogeneous to render the description useless as a guide to action. But its belief that a successful war against Islamist terror required the overthrow of Baathist tyranny in Iraq was justified. The attack on the Twin Towers, and the ease with which a fanatical terrorist group could attack the US mainland and kill thousands of civilians in a single morning, made Saddam's belated removal essential. This remains so even though – indeed more than ever because – we now know the extent of the intelligence failures surrounding his own military capabilities.

We know now that Saddam lacked WMD. But even had our intelligence been better before the war, we should still not have been able to judge the capability of his bellicose and irrational regime to threaten its neighbours and us with such weapons in future, including the near future. Saddam would not comply with what the United Nations Security Council required of him. We do know enough – and did before the war – about internationally mandated inspections that we should be unwilling to rely on them in the case of recalcitrant regimes. Hans Blix, as head of the International Atomic Energy Agency, failed to find evidence of Saddam's nuclear weapons programme in the 1980s and described Iraq's cooperation with the inspectors as 'exemplary'. (Blame for the fact that North Korea could embark undetected on extracting plutonium for use in weapons also rests with Blix.)

In these circumstances, and with this degree of uncertainty, it was important that we invade Iraq and topple Saddam. This was not because he had WMD, but, paradoxically, because he did not have them – at least not in the form in which they were strategically usable – and he wanted them. The point is best appreciated with a comparison often favoured by critics of the Bush Administration. This is the charge that the US and UK were being hypocritical by fighting in Iraq while simultaneously pursuing diplomacy with North Korea. Indeed no less a person than the Democratic challenger for Vice-President in 2004, John Edwards, made this criticism in his campaign, as reported by Reuters:

> The first-term senator…noted that of the three countries singled out by Bush as part of an 'axis of evil' – Iraq, North Korea and Iran – 'you know, we invaded the one of those three that doesn't have nuclear weapons'.

It was a muddle-headed criticism, on many grounds. First, the geo-political position of Saddam's tyranny was different from North Korea's: we have more potential economic leverage over North Korea. Secondly, Saddam was an active supporter of terrorism, both Islamist and secular, making his removal an especially urgent task. Thirdly, the US and UK did not launch a pre-emptive war against Saddam: we had been at war with him for 12 years owing to his continued defiance of the ceasefire agreement that concluded the first Gulf War. Fourthly, and most urgent, we were justified in overthrowing Saddam in order to prevent him from becoming the next Kim Jong-il – no longer a tyrant of scarcely imaginable depravity, but a tyrant of scarcely imaginable depravity with a nuclear capability.

The war's mainstream critics, invoking realist criteria and the fear of unintended consequences of regime change, argued for deterrence and containment in preference to war. Yet even supposing Saddam had been capable of being deterred indefinitely – a premise that his record did not support – the risks of deterrence would have been enormous, despite the West's military superiority. The Soviet Union was effectively deterred during the Cold War, but the Soviet nuclear arsenal conversely deterred the West from assisting in the Hungarian uprising in 1956 and the Prague Spring in 1968. It is not hard to imagine how Saddam, had he been even slightly more rational a political actor, could likewise have become a dominant regional leader.

Effective containment of Saddam would have required continuous mass military deployment on the borders of Iraq and over the no-fly zones; a tightening of economic sanctions;

an inspections regime robust enough – unlike that of Hans Blix – to withstand and outwit Saddam's intimidation, espionage and fraud; and the active support of France and Russia on the UN Security Council. That is, in fact, the premise of the most cogent anti-war case I have come across. It has been made by the philosopher Michael Walzer, who argues:

> [T]he campaign against the war should never have been only an antiwar campaign. It should have been a campaign for a strong international system, designed and organized to defeat aggression, control weapons of mass destruction, stop massacres and ethnic cleansing, and assist in the politics of transition after brutal regimes are overthrown. But an international system of this sort has to be the work of many different states, not of one state.[31]

That is far removed from the actual campaign waged by any significant anti-war organisation in the US and the UK. More to the point, it bears no relation to the way the international order works. However gratuitously abrasive President Bush's diplomacy may have been (and it was) over Iraq, there was no prospect that the international system Walzer describes could have been organised with French or Russian agreement. The only states among the permanent members of the UN Security Council who would be prepared to police such a regime are the US and the UK – exactly the arrangement that did obtain in the Iraq war.

Had we trusted in containment of Saddam, we should one day have woken to an ultimatum from him to transfer Kuwait's oil revenues to a numbered bank account, or else see a nuclear device exploded over Kuwait City. Given the holes in the West's containment policy, the fact that the US does not formally extend its nuclear guarantee to its allies in the region (hence Israel's deliberate ambiguity in stating its own capabilities), and the record of near-suicidal aggression by Baathist Iraq, Saddam's threat would have been credible. Indeed, it would have been credible even if it had been a bluff, given our lack of certain knowledge about his military capabilities. The

only courses then available to the US and its allies would have
been either acquiescence in Saddam's demands in the hope of
buying him off – a policy technically known as appeasement –
or a pre-emptive war fought with doubtful prospect of success.
This is where the analogy with containment of the old
Soviet Union breaks down. We contained the Soviet Union
because we had no other option: the USSR was a nuclear-
armed power, and to confront it militarily was to run a very
high risk of nuclear war. Containment was, moreover, a reasonably stable arrangement because the Soviet leadership –
while totalitarian and expansionist (witness its aggression by
proxy that started the Korean War) – was nonetheless susceptible to traditional deterrence. Saddam was not that type of
minimally rational political agent: he launched three aggressive
wars in 17 years, each of which almost destroyed his regime.[32]
After 9/11, it became urgent to deal with this rogue state
before it became either a failed state or a harbourer of terrorism of unprecedented destructiveness, or both.

**WERE WE WRONG?**

In spite of this, the cost of war – financially and, much more
important, in terms of lives lost – has been greater than the
supporters of regime change generally expected, and certainly
than the US and British governments prepared for. Combined
with the absence of Saddam's WMD and the questions this
raises about Bush and Blair's veracity, this has led many who
originally supported the war to change their minds. Were we
wrong?

We liberal hawks clearly were wrong to have assumed that
intervention would be well planned. But neither did the critics
of the war see their expectations confirmed. The loudest of
them, George Galloway MP, famously harangued US Senators
in May 2005:

> I told the world that Iraq, contrary to your claims, did
> not have weapons of mass destruction. I told the world,
> contrary to your claims, that Iraq had no connection to
> al-Qaeda. I told the world, contrary to your claims, that

Iraq had no connection to the atrocity on 9/11 2001.
I told the world, contrary to your claims, that the Iraqi
people would resist a British and American invasion of
their country and that the fall of Baghdad would not be
the beginning of the end, but merely the end of the
beginning. Senator, in everything I said about Iraq, I
turned out to be right and you turned out to be wrong...[33]

Well, no: Galloway was practising creative elision. He had
in fact predicted not that the fall of Baghdad would be the end
of the beginning, but that overthrowing Saddam would require
Coalition forces 'to destroy the cities in a kind of Dresden-like
bombardment'. A matter of days before Baghdad fell to
Coalition forces, he forecast that 'the entire city will become a
firestorm and that the Iraqis will fight to the end and then
beyond the end'. Galloway's expectation that Iraq's dictator
would be remembered as a second Saladin seemed to be
founded on an erroneous character assessment too: 'I think he
will be the last man standing in the bunker.'[34]

Inferring that Iraqis would fight in defence of a gangster
regime that had destroyed civil society and slaughtered scores
of thousands was a huge assumption that has not been gain-
said by the unpopularity of the post-Saddam occupation. The
Coalition forces *were* treated as liberators: it is the maladroit
occupation that has failed Iraqis, not the overthrow of
Saddam. The 'resistance' – a historically loaded term that
exactly misrepresents the ideology of the Jihadists – is rejected
by the emerging institutions of Iraqi civil society. Abdullah
Muhsin, Foreign Representative of the Iraqi Federation of
Trade Unions (and an opponent of the war) maintains:

Iraq is not another Vietnam; the so-called resistance are no
maquis. The resistance offers at best another dictatorship
modelled on Saddam's regime, at worst an al-Zarqawi-
inspired mediaeval theocracy using Iraq, rather than
Afghanistan, as a base for its war against the US and Arab
regimes. These forces offer only hell to Iraqis and harbour
some of the world's most dangerous ideas. They have no

89

open social or political programme and no popular base, and are feared by most Iraqis. Widespread, popular sentiment against the foreign occupation of our country does not translate into legitimation of these forces.[35]

Among more mainstream opponents of war, the record of predictions was uniformly hopeless. The Liberal Democrats, who have consistently and (among parliamentarians at least) unanimously opposed the Government on the issue, stand out. Jenny Tonge, then the party's International Development spokesman, advised before the war:

> Saddam Hussein is unlikely to sit in his bunker and recite John Benjamin [sic] — 'Come friendly bombs and fall on Slough/Baghdad'. If he has the capability, he will attack his neighbours, probably Israel.[36]

Her party leader, Charles Kennedy, insisted: 'Any war will cause a refugee crisis of huge proportions.'[37] Any other war, perhaps, but not this one: Iraqi civilians, able to distinguish between a war on Baathist totalitarianism and a war on them, stayed put. 'The same [Bush] doctrines could equally be applied by India vis-à-vis Pakistan, or in any dispute where a state feels threatened. It is throwing a match into a barrel of oil', worried Baroness Williams of Crosby, the Lib Dem leader in the House of Lords, shortly before India and Pakistan agreed to talks to resolve the Kashmir dispute.[38]

Bad predictions are not the preserve of one side alone; they are politically promiscuous. But they are not, either, of equal consequence. Opponents of the war would undoubtedly claim that the most egregious failure was that of the Government's intelligence with regard to Saddam's military capabilities. On this, we shall inevitably differ. It seems plausible that Tony Blair persuaded himself of the cogency of the intelligence conclusions about Saddam's WMD, where a more empirically minded person would have demurred. But that is far from the unproved assertion of dishonesty, which has not been substantiated by any formal inquiry, and is inherently unlikely (why fabricate something you know will be shortly refuted?). It is also far from being a disqualification for political office; on this issue, it may be an asset.

No stockpiles of WMD have been found, but that is not the same as an absence of intent.[39] Shortly after the fall of the regime, parts of a nuclear centrifuge were uncovered in a scientist's garden in Iraq.[40] They had been hidden for 12 years in order to evade successive inspections regimes. Weapons inspectors would never have found them, for there is a limit to how many gardens an inspections team can dig up, even supposing the idea were to occur to them in the first place. Christopher Hitchens aptly observed at the time:

> [T]his is not just a 'find' in itself – such gas centrifuges
> are used for the enrichment of uranium – but evidence
> of a larger and wider design to fool the international
> community and to wait for a better day to restart
> Saddam's nuclear program. If you find hard physical
> and documentary evidence, along with a complex plan
> to keep it under wraps, you are entitled to make a few
> presumptions, not including the presumption of innocence.
> Nobody bothers to cover up nothing.[41]

A Prime Minister is not only entitled to make presumptions: he is obliged to, especially on this issue. UN Security Council Resolution 1441 mandated Saddam's immediate and full compliance with weapons inspectors and UN requirements. Demonstrably such compliance was not received and never would have been. The anti-war campaigners maintain there was no connection between 9/11 and Saddam, and in a strict technical sense they are right. But consider the implications. The destruction of the Twin Towers demonstrated that containment of Saddam, quite apart from being a cruel policy imposing punitive sanctions on exactly the wrong target (Iraqis, rather than their oppressor), was also a tenuous one. Someday, unless we act to prevent it, the terrorists will obtain a weapons capability that can kill far more than the 3,000 dead on 9/11.[42] Western governments have the duty to interdict that flow of weapons from their most likely source. In the case of Saddam's regime, war was not even an act of pre-emption; it was an insistence on the terms of the ceasefire agreement that had ended the first Gulf War and on 17 successive UN Security Council resolutions.

To sum up this chapter: we cannot know whether our actions in insisting that Saddam comply with his international obligations or be overthrown have prevented a future disaster. No one – probably not even Saddam – knows the answer to that question. We do know, however, that our enemies have declared war on us, and we have to respond not as agents of law but as wielders of the sword. Failing to recognise this will mean that we refrain from taking the steps necessary to win. Our side did not start the war in Iraq: Saddam did, when he annexed Kuwait in 1990 and then flouted the terms of the ceasefire agreement after his forces had been expelled from the country. Having concluded that war, on our terms and not his, the US and UK governments discharged their obligation to protect their citizens from the most likely conduit for terror conducted with weapons of mass destruction. Even if Iraq fails to become a constitutional democracy, and even if – worse still – the barbarities practised by the Iraqi 'resistance' become an enduring part of the Iraqi political landscape, that central case for war remains. That does not absolve the Bush Administration from its culpable misjudgements and insouciance regarding post-Saddam Iraq – but the achievement that was won in excising a gangster regime from that country and region remains.

1 'Blair hails "ripple of change" in Middle East', *Guardian*, 2 March 2005.
2 'The war's silver lining', Jonathan Freedland, *Guardian*, 2 March 2005.
3 *Strategic Survey 2004/05*, International Institute for Strategic Studies, London, May 2005.
4 Fouad Ajami, 'Autumn of the autocrats', *Foreign Affairs*, May/June 2005, p. 27.
5 See
http://www.whitehouse.gov/news/releases/2005/02/20050202-11.html

6 'Methodist President reflects on Madrid terror', 19 March 2004, at http://www.methodist.org.uk/index.cfm?fuseaction=news.content&cmid=746

7 John Plender, *Going off the Rails: Global Capital and the Crisis of Legitimacy* (Chichester: John Wiley & Sons, 2003), p. 26.

8 Paul Foot, 'A shabby excuse for democracy', *Guardian*, 16 October 2001.

9 Peter Bergen, *Holy War, Inc.* (London: Weidenfeld & Nicolson, 2001), p. 41.

10 'Statement: Jihad against Jews and Crusaders', World Islamic Front, 23 February 1998, included in Barry Rubin and Judith Colp Rubin (eds), *Anti-American Terrorism and the Middle East: A Documentary Reader* (Oxford: Oxford University Press, 2002), p. 150.

11 'Interview with Usama bin Laden', December 1998, included in Rubin and Rubin, *Anti-American Terrorism*, p. 156.

12 Thomas Friedman, 'Yes, but what?', *New York Times*, 5 October 2001.

13 Alan B. Krueger and Jitka Maleckova, *Education, Poverty, Political Violence and Terrorism: Is There a Causal Connection?*, NBER Working Paper No. 9074, July 2002. A non-technical version of the paper was published as 'The economics and the education of suicide bombers: does poverty cause terrorism?', *New Republic*, 24 June 2002.

14 Robert A. Pape, 'The strategic logic of suicide terrorism', *American Political Science Review*, August 2003, available at http://www.comm.cornell.edu/als481/readings/the%20logic%20of%20 suicide%20terrorism.pdf

15 Robert Pape, *Dying to Win: The Strategic Logic of Suicide Terrorism* (New York: Random House, 2005).

16 Luca Ricolfi, 'Palestinians, 1981–2003', in *Making Sense of Suicide Missions*, ed. Diego Gambetta (Oxford: Oxford University Press, 2005), p. 118.

17 Martin Kramer, 'Political science targets suicide terrorism. Bystanders: take cover!', 30 September 2003, at http://www.martinkramer.org/pages/899526/index.htm

18 Benjamin quoted and Hoffman cited in 'Suicide bombs potent tools of terrorists', *Washington Post*, 17 July 2005.

19 'Suicide bombers' "ordinary" lives', BBC News Online, 18 July 2005.

20 Kramer, 'Political science targets suicide terrorism'.

21 Though some are. Almost unbelievably, the former Northern Ireland Secretary Mo Mowlam called in April 2004 for negotiations with al-Qaeda: 'Asked if she could imagine "al-Qaeda and Osama bin Laden arriving at the negotiating table," she replied: "You have to do that.

If you do not you condemn large parts of the world to war forever."'
The reason large parts of the world are condemned to war is,
in fact, that radical Islamists declare it. See
http://news.bbc.co.uk/1/hi/uk_politics/3611805.stm
for a report of Dr Mowlam's comments.
22 In a diatribe broadcast on al-Jazeera on 3 November 2001, bin Laden
declared: 'Let us examine the stand of the West and the United Nations
in the developments in Indonesia when they moved to divide the largest
country in the Islamic world in terms of population. This criminal,
Kofi Annan, was speaking publicly and putting pressure on the
Indonesian government, telling it: You have 24 hours to divide and
separate East Timor from Indonesia. Otherwise, we will be forced to
send in military forces to separate it by force. The crusader Australian
forces were on Indonesian shores, and in fact they landed to separate
East Timor, which is part of the Islamic world.' The full text is at
http://news.bbc.co.uk/1/hi/world/monitoring/media_reports/1636782.stm
23 'This was followed by a war of genocide in Bosnia in sight and hearing
of the entire world in the heart of Europe. For several years our brothers
have been killed, our women have been raped, and our children have
been massacred in the safe havens of the United Nations and with its
knowledge and cooperation.' *Ibid.*
24 For example, 'The future of SMs will largely depend on whether,
rather than a crude policy of war and intensifying the clangour of the
clash of civilizations, opportunities for astute policing and genuine
political processes will be taken up in earnest.' Diego Gambetta,
'Can we make sense of suicide missions?', in Gambetta (ed.),
*Making Sense of Suicide Missions*, p. 299.
25 Conor Cruise O'Brien, *Ancestral Voices: Religion and Nationalism
in Ireland* (Dublin: Poolbeg Press, 1994), p. 146.
26 Noam Chomsky, 'The new war against terror', speech delivered at
MIT, 18 October 2001, transcript at
http://www.zmag.org/GlobalWatch/chomskymit.htm
27 UNHCR Briefing, 'Rebuilding lives in Afghanistan', at
http://www.unhcr.ch/cgi-bin/texis/vtx/afghan?page=home
28 By Marc Herold, an Associate Professor of Economics and – of all
things – Women's Studies at the University of New Hampshire. His survey
of Afghan casualties is at
http://pubpages.unh.edu/~mwherold/
29 See, for example, John Pilger, 'This war of lies goes on', *Daily Mirror*,
16 November 2001.

30 On the civilian death toll, see Richard Beeston, 'Iraqis soldier on without power, water, jobs, sewers', *The Times*, 13 May 2005, reporting on a survey for the UN Development Programme entitled *Iraq Living Conditions Survey 2004*.

31 Michael Walzer, 'Can there be a moral foreign policy?', in E. J. Dionne, Jean Bethke Elshtain and Kayla Drogosz (eds), *Liberty and Power: A Dialogue on Religion and US Foreign Policy in an Unjust World*, (Washington: The Brookings Institution, 2004), p. 50.

32 Against Iran under the Shah in 1974, Iran under the Ayatollahs in 1980, and Kuwait in 1990.

33 'Galloway v the US Senate: transcript of statement', *The Times*, 18 May 2005.

34 Galloway's comments are from 'Galloway warns of "street by street, house by house" resistance to US invasion', *IraqJournal.org*, 11 October 2002, at
http://www.iraqjournal.org/journals/021011.html
and Marie Woolf, 'George Galloway: Labour maverick who's a target for Blairites and "The Sun"', *Independent*, 7 April 2003.

35 Abdullah Muhsin, 'We are nobody's pawns', *Guardian*, 23 October 2004.

36 Jenny Tonge, 'The world after September 11', 1 October 2002, at
http://www.jennytonge.org.uk/speeches/1.html

37 'Kennedy attacks Azores summit', BBC News Online, 16 March 2003.

38 'Williams attacks Bush "cabal"', *Guardian*, 23 September 2002.

39 Weapons of mass destruction (WMD), like many portmanteau descriptions, is unhelpful because of its imprecision, but it has come into common use.

40 'White House: centrifuge parts back case on Iraq', CNN, 27 June 2003, at
http://edition.cnn.com/2003/US/06/26/sprj.irq.white.house/

41 Christopher Hitchens, 'Saddahmer Hussein', *Slate.com*, 7 July 2003, at
http://slate.msn.com/id/2085263/

42 Clearly there is great uncertainty about how close terrorists are to acquiring that capability, or how easy it would be for them to launch a devastating attack on a Western country using non-conventional weapons. There are formidable technical difficulties to using such a weapon, even supposing a terrorist group were able to acquire one. There has never been a successful biological attack by terrorists; biological agents need to be spread if they are to be effective, and this depends on climatic factors not within the control of the terrorists.

The chemical attack by the Aum Shinri Kyo cult in Japan using sarin poison gas against commuters in 1995 caused 'only' 12 deaths, and even then depended for its effectiveness on being attempted in the confined space of an underground station. But against that, the prospect of a terrorist group obtaining enriched uranium, smuggling it into the US (or the UK), fashioning it into a crude nuclear weapon, and causing colossal damage is by no means fanciful. The risks, and the preventive actions available to us, are cogently presented by Graham Allison in *Nuclear Terrorism: The Ultimate Preventable Catastrophe* (New York: Henry Holt and Company, 2004) and in the same author's 'How to stop nuclear terror', *Foreign Affairs*, January/February 2004. Allison's 'bet is 9/11 was a striking and dramatic but actually modest introduction to what we will come to know as a grave new world' (see his remarks at http://www.wmassociation.com/reports/spkers/allison.html).

# CHAPTER 4

# THE TASK FOR THE LEFT

*The differences between conservatives and liberals, when the terms are reasonably construed, are family differences among adherents of a free society, defined as one whose institutions ultimately rest on the consent of those affected by their operations. When the security of a free society is threatened by aggressive totalitarianism, these differences must be temporarily subordinated to the common interest in its survival. There is always the danger that in the ever-present and sometimes heated struggles between liberals and conservatives, each group may come to fear the other more than their common enemy. If and when that happens, the darkness of what Marx called 'Asiatic despotism', in modern dress to be sure, will descend upon the world.*

Sidney Hook, 'A Critique of Conservatism'
Address to Social Democrats USA, 1976

## THE PHENOMENON OF BLAIRISM

Events in the Middle East have had an unexpectedly (because indirectly) powerful impact on British politics. The 2005 general election was widely assumed beforehand to be an uninteresting contest with a foregone conclusion. The return of a third-term Labour Government was never in serious doubt, but the manner of that victory is likely to have an enduring influence on the tenor of British foreign policy. Labour suffered heavy losses, with a 100-seat decline in its parliamentary majority. Even then, its parliamentary majority of 67 obscured the weakness of its electoral position, with a share of the vote of just 36 per cent. The issue of the Iraq War contributed to some spectacular electoral upsets in formerly safe Labour seats, notably Hornsey & Wood Green and Manchester Withington, lost to the Liberal Democrats, and Bethnal Green & Bow, lost to a notorious apologist for Saddam Hussein's regime, George Galloway. By having weakened the authority of Tony Blair, the election may also represent an enduring setback to an ambitious attempt to refashion British social democracy.

Those outcomes were not expected. Blair is the most successful leader in the Labour Party's history, and the dominant centrist politician in Europe over the past decade. On becoming Labour leader in 1994, he took a party that had lost four successive general elections – in one of which it almost came third in the popular vote – and secured for it landslide victories. In the early 1980s, when Blair entered Parliament, Labour might conceivably have gone the way of the French Communist Party. A once mighty trade union-based organisation had failed to adapt to social change and was ruinously insistent on doctrinal purity; electoral humiliation, with the party driven back to its regional redoubts, predictably followed.

Blair's approach was not so much to reform the party as to replace it. The auguries were not good. In order to become a party of government, the German Social Democrats (SPD) had ostentatiously abandoned their Marxist ideological antecedents in the 1950s. Labour in the 1990s required a similar symbolic break with the past. Yet the party had always drawn on more eclectic philosophical roots than its European counterparts (Morgan Phillips, once the party's General Secretary, famously remarked that the party owed more to Methodism than to Marxism). Paradoxically this had made it more resistant to change. An obviously outmoded ideology at least has the advantage of a set of definable propositions. Labour's mythology, grounded in the totems of the National Health Service and a socialised economy, was less amenable to reasoned reassessment.

Blair's historic achievement was to force change on the party regardless. In his first speech as leader, at the Labour Party conference in 1994, he showed he understood the importance of symbols. As Tony Benn confided in his diary: 'It was a clever speech. Of course, by attacking Marx and saying he would end Clause 4, Blair opened up a huge and unnecessary debate within the party, in the hope of isolating the left and making them look like troublemakers.'[1]

Apart from the adjective 'unnecessary', this was not far wrong. It is an extraordinary fact that at the end of the twentieth century Labour needed to be told that the immiseration of the proletariat under capitalism had not taken place – that indeed the opposite had happened – and that abolishing property rights was incompatible with liberty and efficiency. Previous Labour leaders, with the exception of Hugh Gaitskell, had treated Clause 4 of Labour's constitution (which specified the aim of the common ownership of the means of production, distribution and exchange) as a historical idiosyncrasy. Blair saw its removal as essential in signalling Labour's acceptance of the market economy.

Yet symbolism apart, New Labour's ideology was notoriously difficult to pin down in its early years (and, many would say, in government too). This was particularly true in foreign policy, of which Blair had little experience. The party formed close links with the Clinton White House, but these were primarily to do with party organisation and strategy.

Up until Clinton's first victory in 1992, the Democrats had lost five out of the six presidential elections since 1968. Even the exceptional win – Jimmy Carter's in 1976 – had been a close-run thing against a Republican candidate enfeebled by the legacy of his predecessor's Watergate scandals. Clinton, a candidate of a new generation, running as a 'New Democrat' of moderate views, was seen by New Labour as a precedent for its own rejuvenation. The strained relations between Clinton and John Major's Conservative Government – over the latter's assistance to the first President Bush in the 1992 campaign, and its feckless approach to the Bosnian crisis – contributed to a presumption of affinity between Clinton and Blair.

Yet New Labour's approach to foreign policy was distinctive only to the extent that it was unrecognisable from the anti-nuclear rhetoric and policies on which the party had campaigned in the 1980s. A belated return to the mainstream was an achievement of sorts, but a negative one: it closed off the most obvious and fruitful line of Conservative attack against Labour. There was scant new thinking in New Labour's foreign and defence policies. More obvious was a longstanding characteristic of Blairism or the 'Third Way': the unstated assumption that all desirable outcomes were compatible, and that the task of government was to realise those outcomes rather than choose among them.

The 1996 party programme and pre-manifesto, *New Labour, New Life for Britain*, thus asserted, with scarcely a nod to recent countervailing history, that 'Labour believes in strong defence'. It envisaged that Britain under a Labour Government would be 'active members of Nato', and of the Allied Rapid Reaction Force; support 'an enhanced role for Western European Union'; retain Britain's independent nuclear deterrent, the Trident missiles; but 'ensure British nuclear weapons are included (eventually) in multilateral negotiations', and support a Comprehensive Test Ban Treaty. Interestingly, there was a strong stated commitment to the Commonwealth but no mention at all of the United States or of the notion of a special relationship. The 1997 election manifesto was similarly reticent on transatlantic relations.[2] It was a manifesto for safety, neutralising foreign affairs as an election issue under an attractive new leader with minimal experience in the field and little evidence of interest in it.

Conventional wisdom holds that a political leader will gain interest in foreign affairs as his domestic reputation diminishes. The contrast between Mrs Thatcher's public stature abroad and at home – revered in both the Soviet Union and the United States, while steadily becoming an electoral liability for the Conservatives in the UK – is the obvious precedent. Tony Blair does not follow it, however. As his critics on the Left point out, Blair's premiership has been marked from the outset by a willingness to commit British troops to action overseas. One well-received (and well-sourced) critical study devoted itself to explaining the conundrum that such a premier, unlike any of his recent predecessors, had deployed troops five times in six years – in Iraq, Kosovo, Sierra Leone, Afghanistan and Iraq again.[3] What makes the record all the more distinctive is that, unlike Mrs Thatcher's successful prosecution of the Falklands campaign, Blair's wars were highly unlikely to deliver electoral dividends. They were campaigns pursued with no certainty of success (especially in Kosovo, where military and journalistic opinion held that only a commitment of ground troops could rebuff Serb aggression), and the potential to cause him substantial electoral damage even if the military outcome were successful. This is, in the case of Iraq in 2003, precisely what did happen. Having dominated the political landscape for a decade, as Mrs Thatcher did before him, Blair lost not only popularity – as also happened to Mrs Thatcher – but, in the 2005 general election, authority as well.

Yet Blair's voluntary sacrifice of Labour's dominance and his own public standing was, in an ill-fated phrase, a price worth paying. There are strong moral and prudential grounds for the Western democracies to pursue an interventionist foreign policy of confronting tyranny and promoting global democracy. Blair did not squander his political dominance of the previous decade: he spent it wisely, in a just, necessary and progressive cause.

## AN ANTI-TOTALITARIAN CAUSE
Argument about the Iraq war is generally framed in consequentialist terms – whether the removal of an appalling regime is an outcome that justifies the civilian casualties; whether Saddam's removal hastens or hinders political reform in the Arab world, and so on. I have argued in this way, too, in the previous chapter. But these debates are necessarily inconclusive for both advocates and opponents of war, because we cannot properly assess what the consequences would have been of allowing Saddam to remain in power.

But there is another route to the case for regime change. There are some issues in politics that are irreducible because they express our deepest values. Most liberals who are opposed to capital punishment would continue to oppose it even if it could be reliably shown that the death penalty deterred potential murderers. We find the very idea of judicial execution an affront to liberal values. This is not to say it must always be avoided no matter what (it is difficult to argue that the Nuremberg sentences were unjust); there is, however, an immediate and overwhelming presumption against it. On a much higher order of historical importance and potential suffering, few observers in 1940 doubted the near certainty of military defeat under Churchill; yet the likely alternative of a government headed by Lord Halifax that aimed to settle with Nazi Germany in return for nominal sovereignty would still have been morally unconscionable.

Normally in political argument a comparison to Nazi Germany obscures more than it illuminates. But I choose it deliberately in this case because the Syrian founders of the Baath Party, who were educated at the Sorbonne in the 1930s, were strongly influenced by the fascist ideology they encountered in Europe, and Saddam's regime was modelled on both Hitler and Stalin. It is an apt comparison, save only for the fact that Baathist Iraq did not imminently threaten us. (The threat was not imminent, but it was inevitable.) Deliberately allowing such a regime to remain in place when we had the power to remove it would have been to violate values that are axiomatic. That is not to say it would be right to overthrow a bestial regime regardless of any other considerations, ever; there would, however, be a presumption in favour of such action where it was possible.

I argued in the previous chapter that the analogy of containment of the Soviet Union does not hold in the case of Saddam Hussein. Containment of the Soviets was reasonably stable, containment of Saddam was steadily eroding. Direct military confrontation with the Soviet Union risked a nuclear war; we had the ability to overthrow Saddam without undertaking excessive risks to ourselves, to the benefit of Iraq's people and our allies in the region. On prudential grounds there was a strong case for overthrowing Saddam. Given that premise, we should have been morally at fault in not pursuing that course, which accorded with values that are axiomatic to liberalism.

It is worth being specific about those values. Intervention in Iraq was not strictly a 'humanitarian war': it was an anti-totalitarian war. It was a war for the cause of liberty, there being a literal and not merely a metaphorical sense that liberty in an international order threatened by theocratic fanaticism is indivisible.

In his book *Terror and Liberalism*, the left-wing writer Paul Berman also locates Islamist terrorism's place in the tradition of totalitarian nihilist ideology, and concludes: 'We are the anti-nihilists...In the anti-nihilist system, freedom for others means safety for ourselves. Let us be for the freedom of others.'[4] This seems to me an ideal capsule description of the task of the Left today, stemming directly from values of anti-fascism and internationalist solidarity. Secular Baathism and Islamist totalitarianism are the natural enemies of the Left, and the task of uprooting them and replacing them with constitutional government is our natural cause.

One thoughtful writer on the Right who recognises this ideological consistency while challenging its premises is the *Times* columnist and former Conservative MP Matthew Parris. He argues:

> To the liberal interventionist, the thought never occurs
> that Saddam Hussein might have been a product of
> the whole Iraqi people and their history, as well as an
> imposition upon them. They think that he was only
> an imposition and in their hearts the people know it.
> Remove him, thinks the interventionist, and they will
> love us. If at first they do not rise and hail us then
> another heave is called for: one last heave.[5]

This is parody, but it needs to be taken seriously. It is true that liberal interventionists would be unwise to expound democracy as a universal solvent. Democracy may also be the tool of the illiberal (as would be the case if, say, Islamists were to win elections in Iraq and use their governing position to ensure that none ever took place again).

This perception of a discontinuity between liberalism and democracy is argued by Fareed Zakaria in a stimulating recent book.[6] Zakaria maintains that the spread of democracy internationally has not corresponded to a spread of liberty. That is because the essence of a free society is not popular control, but liberal institutions: the rule of law, property rights and freedom from arbitrary authority. It is an important distinction. First it identifies some of the limits of democratic organisation (for example, in the advanced industrial economies monetary policy is now typically insulated – through independent central banks – from political control, and thereby serves much better the aims of liberalism). Secondly, it provides a guide to what is most likely to be effective in an interventionist foreign policy.

Conservatives dismiss the notion of what they contemptuously term 'nation-building'. President Bush did so in the presidential debates in the 2000 campaign, implicitly favouring withdrawal from important US commitments such as the Balkans. They have a minor point here. Nations are cohesive entities with coherent historical memories, and take generations to evolve. What we can do, however, is build not nations but states – collections of institutions that protect the people from capricious rule and violence. In Iraq that is a limited but essential goal; moreover, it *is* a universal principle. Polities may be more or less democratic, or not democratic at all. But there is no society in which Saddam's tyranny would be anything other than an 'imposition', because it was utterly brutal. It was not a polity at all, but a gangster regime.

Whether or not Iraq becomes a stable democracy in the Middle East is uncertain (though I am hopeful, even confident, because there is already a functioning example of a constitutional democracy in Iraqi Kurdistan, and because of the astonishing courage of Iraqis in turning out to vote despite intimidation by Jihadists). But, at a minimum, Iraq can be a state where essential requirements of political order and constitutionalism are observed.[7]

Moreover, the Left has a particular input to make on what those requirements comprise. First, *even though* it is possible to argue for intervention while holding to Zakaria's Burkean scepticism about instilling democracy, there are grounds for being more ambitious. Zakaria is right to observe that liberal societies owe more to the Roman tradition (specifically in law) than the Greek (democracy was never practised on a wide scale, and in the city-states was even then severely attenuated), and that deliberative democracy often requires the insulation of decision-making from popular pressures. Yet conservative scepticism has inconsistencies of its own. As the political theorist Stephen Holmes has argued, in a review of Zakaria's book:

> [E]ven if we grant that liberal constitutionalism ought to take priority [over democracy], we need a way of establishing it, and Zakaria never adequately explains how that is to be accomplished. In certain passages he comes close to implying that mere political will is enough, as when he suggests that moderate politics could be brought to Kazakhstan simply by crafting a better constitution. But the formal provisions of constitutions cannot create a politics without regard to the forces operating in society; the rule of law itself needs social support and cannot be built from scratch, or against the grain, by political will.[8]

The requirement for social support is an argument the Left must advance. A liberal state is not necessarily a lightly governed state, and the task of constructing a viable Iraqi democracy will be made easier if social policies are geared to eliciting the consent of the governed. Reconstruction of Iraq is not best left to a model of unregulated markets and minimal welfare provision. As the historian Brian Brivati has argued in the context of Iraq:

> Central and eastern Europe teach us that neoliberal models do not achieve democratic consolidations, but social-market models do. A free-market approach to welfare and wealth distribution produces instability. If you develop slowly, use welfare capitalism and build consensus, you consolidate quicker.[9]

Even if you believe that free markets produce greater material wealth, it is wrong to maintain that the successful export of democracy to non-Western countries requires the introduction of capitalism (consider the still highly regulated economy of India) or a certain level of material wealth (consider Mali, a democratic country with an adult literacy rate of less than 26 per cent and a life expectancy of 49 years[10]).

In arguments about the export of democracy, there are encouraging precedents. Burkeans of an earlier generation claimed – especially during the ill-fated Weimar republic – that democracy was not merely Western but specifically Anglo-Saxon. Yet German culture and politics turned out to be far from inherently authoritarian. A democratic polity was founded after the war, and West Germany's political leaders (Adenauer on the Right, and the Social Democrat leader Kurt Schumacher) immediately instilled in it a form of politics that was pro-Western, anti-totalitarian and free of xenophobia. The earlier tradition of the SPD was Marxist, and that of German conservatism was the *Sonderbewusstsein* (a special consciousness hostile to liberal values), yet no trace now remains in mainstream German politics of those elements.

President Bush is a man the Left can and ought to work with, largely because he does not evince much conservative scepticism about the merits of democracy and its export. This is an important development in post-war American policy. The traditional weakness of American containment policy in the Cold War – a just cause pursued with varying degrees of resolution by post-war presidents but with ultimate success – was its willingness to ally with authoritarian governments in order to resist Communist totalitarianism.

It is easy to overstate the degree of *realpolitik* in American foreign policy in this period. The pursuit of a stable balance of power had some horrendous casualties, as when the Ford Administration acquiesced in Indonesia's invasion (and subsequent annexation) of East Timor in 1975. But it was also consistent with, in the same year, the signing of the Helsinki Final Act, which served to undermine the legitimacy of Soviet Communism by focusing attention on human rights.[11] The famous distinction of convenience made by Jeane Kirkpatrick, President Reagan's first ambassador to the UN, between authoritarian regimes, with whom the US could work, and totalitarian ones was never consistently observed.

But even Ronald Reagan, the most Wilsonian of post-war Presidents, was susceptible to traditional balance-of-power approaches in attaining US goals. A deservedly notorious example was the tilt to Saddam's Iraq in order to contain the militancy of revolutionary Iran. In retrospect – and at the time, come to that – this was not only morally reprehensible but also ran counter to the aims it was designed to serve. To have an aggressive and expansionist genocidal tyrant seeking to augment his oil wealth and influence in that region was a disastrous policy on grounds of *realpolitik* alone. Reagan was also acutely sensitive to the notion of projecting force, especially after a massive bomb killed 242 US servicemen in Beirut in 1983. He intervened directly only in limited actions, such as Grenada in 1983.

Bush's innovation is to recognise the limits of realism. In the realist model, states are often compared to billiard balls: the ball's internal composition is opaque and unimportant; what matters is how the ball interacts with others on the table. The model's great weakness is its failure to address the power of ideas. By contrast, Bush seeks to advance US foreign policy goals with an axiom that is idealistic but also has academic support. The axiom of Bush's strategic doctrine is that the spread of liberty, not the search for allies in an eternally shifting balance of power, is the guarantor of American and Western security. It is a radical notion, for it prescribes a deep engagement in external affairs, and – despite European condescension towards the cowboy in the White House – an intellectually coherent one. If it was not poverty that drove a group of well-educated and affluent Saudis to slam aeroplanes into office blocks and government buildings that September morning in 2001, but the lack of an outlet for dissidence in Arab societies other than through religious fanaticism, then there is a pragmatic case for making the spread of democracy the central goal of foreign policy.

## CONVERGENCE OF ISOLATIONISMS
This elision of a traditional division between the pursuit of ideals and the exercise of power is almost unprecedented in

American foreign policy, while at the same time being a distinctively American approach. Only Tony Blair among non-American statesmen adopts similar language so readily, as in his address to Congress in July 2003:

> The spread of freedom is the best security for the free.
> It is our last line of defence and our first line of attack.
> Just as the terrorist seeks to divide humanity in hate,
> so we have to unify it around an idea and that that [sic]
> idea is liberty. We must find the strength to fight for this
> idea; and the compassion to make it universal.[12]

It is the great irony of modern politics that this doctrine should be opposed, indeed sneered at, and for classically realist reasons, by people who are typically regarded as being on the Left. This became clear when Serb aggression against Bosnia's democracy in the early 1990s produced a remarkable coincidence of view between European conservatives and an increasingly isolationist Left. Here, for example, is what Noam Chomsky (again) had to say in his 1994 book of interviews, *The Prosperous Few and the Restless Many*, when asked about a possible military counter to Serb aggression and genocide in Bosnia:

> It's not only a moral issue – you have to ask about
> the consequences, and they could be quite complex.
> What if a Balkan war were set off? One consequence
> is that conservative military forces within Russia could
> move in...At that point you're getting fingers on nuclear
> weapons involved. It's also entirely possible that an attack
> on the Serbs, who feel that they're the aggrieved party,
> could inspire them to move more aggressively in Kosovo,
> the Albanian area. That could set off a large-scale war,
> with Greece and Turkey involved. So it's not so simple.
> Or what if the Bosnian Serbs, with the backing of both
> the Serbian and maybe even other Slavic regions, started
> a guerrilla war? Western military 'experts' have suggested
> it could take a hundred thousand troops just to more or
> less hold the area. Maybe so.

So one has to ask a lot of questions about consequences. Bombing Serbian gun emplacements sounds simple, but you have to ask how many people are going to end up being killed. That's not so simple.[13]

With the sole exception – which was itself a reason for adopting the opposite approach to that urged by Chomsky – of Serb aggression in Kosovo, all of these prognostications turned out to be wrong. The issue did turn out to be simple enough in one crucial respect a year after the book was published. In August 1995 the Croats began a ground offensive against the Serbs, while Nato launched air attacks against Serb positions after the shelling of the Sarajevo marketplace. The resulting rapid and decisive shift in territorial advantage against the Serbs enabled the negotiation of the Dayton Accords. Chomsky's warnings had proved groundless. Had Nato followed the advice of this paragon of radical conscience and dissent, much needless suffering would have ensued.

Though his supporters would not appreciate the comparison, Chomsky's approach accorded with that of the Conservative Government of John Major between 1992 and 1995. British policy over Bosnia comprised little more than a conservative pessimism concerning the ability to exercise power for humanitarian purposes in the international order. (Memorably, Malcolm Rifkind, then Defence Secretary and later Foreign Secretary, rejected the proposal in 1994 of US Senator Bob Dole for a lifting of the arms embargo with the words: 'You Americans don't know the horrors of war.' His American interlocutor had been nearly killed and permanently disabled in World War II.[14])

It is appropriate that the principal architects of the Bosnian betrayal, Douglas Hurd (the Foreign Secretary) and Rifkind, should more recently have opposed regime change in Baghdad and sought the early withdrawal of British forces. But it is extraordinary that many of the conservative rationalisations for non-intervention in successive humanitarian wars – Bosnia, Kosovo, Afghanistan and Iraq – should find a counterpart on the Left. Progressives should be opposing the obscurantist, isolationist and amoral elements of conservatism; what they have done since the Cold War is frequently oppose for opposition's sake, and they thereby find themselves the voice of reaction. In foreign policy the Left discredits itself if the only cause it can find is a reflexive opposition to whatever the United States does.

The Left's refusal to assess US policy on its merits could not have come at a less apt time. Post-war American foreign policy has been compromised by tactical alliances with authoritarian regimes. While defenders of this record could point to South Korea or Taiwan as instances of authoritarian allies of the US that made the transition to democracy, there are numerous counterexamples of authoritarian allies that ossified in their repression. President Bush, by contrast, maintains that the spread of liberty, not the balance of power among states, is the best assurance for Western security. His reasoning explains a distinctive stance on the Arab–Israeli conflict that has been lost on many of his European critics: pressing for internal reform in the Palestinian Authority, while being the first US President to aim explicitly for a Palestinian state.

Bush's foreign policy principles are credible. A state that oppresses the people under its domestic jurisdiction is unlikely to be open and trustworthy on the international stage. In a world where Islamist terrorists, rogue states and weapons of mass destruction may come together to pose new threats, our values and interests coincide in promoting democracy internationally. The cause of regime change is not *merely* a liberal cause in contradiction to a strained conservative pessimism: it is a prudent reading of the threats Western societies face when those bellicose elements are caucuses rather than states. But it is still a defining issue for the Left, and one that few in Britain other than the Prime Minister have properly appreciated.

## THE TOTALITARIAN TEMPTATION

One of the reasons for the obduracy of the Left over the cause of regime change goes beyond mere conservative pessimism, however. As in earlier episodes of anti-totalitarian struggle, there are disturbing indications that parts of the Left stand

THE TASK FOR THE LEFT

with the other side. In British politics, these elements make up the Stop the War Coalition and its successor organisation, the Respect Coalition.

'Respect' has an ideological character derived from the organisation that largely established and controls it, the Trotskyite Socialist Workers' Party (SWP). An American precedent would be the Progressive Party, under whose auspices Henry Wallace ran for the White House in 1948. Ostensibly devoted to a foreign policy of accommodation and cooperation with the Soviet Union, the Progressive Party is known to have been a Communist front. But there is a difference, in that the SWP operates in tactical alliance with the cause of Islamist militancy. Its political ally is a fringe organisation called the Muslim Association of Britain (MAB).

MAB was founded in 1997 by the London-based spokesman for the Muslim Brotherhood. It was a co-sponsor with the Stop the War Coalition of the million-strong anti-war protest in Hyde Park in February 2003. It has both advanced anti-Semitism itself and promoted the cause of anti-Semites. In 2000, it published in its newsletter a notorious anti-Semitic forgery supposedly penned by Benjamin Franklin, but actually the work of an American Nazi in the 1930s.[15] After Israel assassinated the Hamas leader Abdel Aziz Rantissi in 2004, the MAB issued a press release describing him as 'a doctor of medicine, father and statesman fighting for the rights of Palestinian people across the globe, [who] will be sorely missed'. He was, apart from any other activity, a Holocaust denier who counted the annihilation of six million Jews one of 'the lies of the Zionists'.[16]

The *Observer* and *New Statesman* columnist Nick Cohen commented on this peculiar alliance:

> Why is a British socialist group forming a political
> alliance with repressive, Islamic fundamentalists?
> Because it really is exceedingly stupid...The enemies
> of political freedom and the enemies of religious and
> sexual freedom are at one, and will soon be presenting
> joint candidates to the electorate.[17]

There is something bizarre in a coalition of the far Left and theocratic reaction,[18] but I would dispute that this is merely opportunism. There is an ideological consistency at work, and it mirrors the pro-fascism found among some on the far Left – mostly in France, but also in Britain – in the 1930s. Many intellectual forebears and political leaders of fascism have come from the Left (notably Georges Sorel and Benito Mussolini), and some unambiguously pro-fascist parties have sprung from the Left and considered themselves part of the Left. Most prominent among those parties was the Parti Populaire Français established by the Communist leader Jacques Doriot in 1936, on which the short-lived British People's Party was modelled. Ideas from certain parts of the Left have also long been assimilated into fascist ideology. The most interesting historical figure in this respect is the Belgian Marxist Henri de Man, whose ideas were a powerful influence on Mussolini, and also on a generation of French Socialists led by Marcel Déat. Déat founded successive pro-fascist parties in the 1930s and under Vichy – which he strongly opposed on the grounds that it was insufficiently accommodating to the Nazi occupiers.[19]

There is, therefore, some precedent for the extraordinary fact that the SWP urged victory for the regime of Saddam Hussein in the Iraq War[20] and now supports a 'Resistance' that itself is an arm of the former Baathist regime and its Islamist allies.[21] Even in allying with theocratic Islamist reaction the SWP is following where the British National Party has led. The BNP leader, Nick Griffin, was secretly filmed in 2001 rousing his supporters with anti-Muslim demagoguery, but in the late 1980s he was a prominent advocate of a current in European fascism known as the 'Political Soldiers'. This group gained its intellectual ballast from the doctrines of the Italian fascist theorist Giulio Evola and its historical inspiration from the Romanian Iron Guard. Its cult of violence was expressed in support for the Islamic Republics of Iran and Libya.[22]

This episode of far Left alliance with fascism is unusual, and it is pernicious, but it is not novel.

## LAW NOT WAR?

Disregarding the totalitarian wing of the Left, there is a powerful objection among liberals to an interventionist foreign policy. This is that interventionism disregards the civilising influence of international law. Though about law, this is not a legalistic argument. It is influenced by the writings of the international lawyer Philippe Sands in a recent book, *Lawless World – America and the Making and Breaking of Global Rules.* Sands stresses that a rules-based international order is an essential feature of civilised norms, and believes the Bush Administration's unilateralism stands in contrast to the ethos of US foreign policy since World War II:

> Imperfect as the rules of international law may be,
> they are necessary and they reflect minimum standards
> of acceptable behaviour. They provide a standard for
> judging the legitimacy of international actions.[23]

Sands believes in adhering to rules, even where they generate the 'wrong' result. Thus, while he opposed the Iraq War, he would have gone along with it had there been proper authority from the UN Security Council.[24] He argues: 'We have rules for a reason...They may sometimes produce an unsatisfactory result, but that doesn't mean one of the parties to the dispute is able to decide unilaterally that the rule no longer should apply.'[25]

A liberal application of Sands's argument would hold that a world without rules is one in which disputes are decided by the threat of superior force. By definition, superior force inheres in the stronger powers. A progressive politics would strengthen legal recourses to the settlement of disputes, and reinforce the rule of law by insisting that the strong, as well as the weak, adhere to it.

This is an important objection, and international law is an important construct. In some fields (such as international trade and payments) it has done discernible good in constraining the exercise of arbitrary power and subjecting the international order to a greater sense of fairness and non-discrimination. (One example would be the first major ruling of the World

Trade Organization, in 1997, which ruled against the US for applying stricter rules on the chemical characteristics of imported petroleum than it did for domestically refined petroleum.[26]) The tempering of national sovereignty by a rules-based system is an attractive vision for a progressive politics. It is one that accords with a particular conception of the nature of international legitimacy that is especially common in continental Europe. This holds that the state arbitrates between competing claims to secure the common good, and does so in an autonomous space apart from the partial interests of the state's citizens. Americans, meanwhile, tend to have a Lockean suspicion of the notion of a collective good separate from the individual interests of those who make up that body. In the American view, the sole criterion of the interests of the state is the collective views of its members, democratically expressed.[27]

I am not competent to discuss the legality of the Iraq War, but arguments about the role of international law in relations between states ought not to be left to lawyers alone. In particular, the American unease at the notion of a rules-based system that stands outside and above politics is not groundless or reactionary.

The rules are a human construct, and what rules we set and how we enforce them require political judgements. An example is the trend in many advanced industrial economies to make monetary policy subject to a rules-based system of inflation targeting. The decision on what the target should be is set (in the case of the UK) by the Chancellor of the Exchequer; it is a political decision. The responsibility for meeting that target is the responsibility of the central bank; that is an operational decision. A problem arises when a rules-based system is seen as something apart from this political source of legitimacy, as when pressure groups seek to use international law as a means of overturning what are essentially political decisions, which are the responsibility of elected governments rather than an unelected judiciary.

This is more than a normative claim about where sovereignty should lie: it is also a pragmatic observation about the nature of international relations. International law is not like domestic law in a constitutional democracy, in which there is a universally accepted set of conventions and statutes that is applicable to everyone and that may be enforced against anyone who breaks it. The international order, unlike a constitutional democracy, is anarchic: there is no supranational body that exercises sovereignty and that thereby has the power to implement law. Regardless of whether that is a good or a bad thing (I think it is a good thing), it is an inevitable feature of modern international politics: the more a state, by virtue of the spread of democratic government, is responsive to the mores and customs of its people, the less likely it will be to cede sovereignty to a higher body.

We can anticipate the trouble that an unreflective appeal to international law will create by looking at the submission of one pressure group, Greenpeace, in lobbying against the Iraq War. (Its submission was written by Duncan Currie, a New Zealand-based barrister.) Greenpeace argued:

> The new Bush doctrine of 'preventive war' which
> was published in the National Security Strategy in
> September 2002 contemplates attacking a state in
> the absence of specific evidence of a pending attack.
> This doctrine marks a departure from the prohibition
> of the use of force under international law, starting
> from the Kellogg–Briand pact, the establishment of
> the Nuremberg Charter, the conclusion of the
> United Nations Charter and the establishment of the
> International Criminal Court, and marks a return to
> a readiness to use force in international relations.[28]

The Kellogg–Briand Pact of 1928 was a declaration committing signatory states to renounce war for all time. It was negotiated by a US Secretary of State, Frank Kellogg, who devoted his entire period of office to securing more than 30 international arbitration and conciliation agreements; it was signed by almost every independent state then in existence. It is, as the author of the Greenpeace brief points out, still in force. And therein lies the danger of this line of reasoning.

The Pact proved valueless in restraining, let alone defeating, dictators bent on invading, annexing and plundering other states. It was obviously useless against Italian and Japanese aggression in Abyssinia and Manchuria, and became still more completely discredited by Nazi aggression and genocide in succeeding years. Yet to this day it remains the talisman and crowning achievement of the peace movement. That must yield a political judgement on the peace movement's schemes for sublimating conflict in international law.

International law is not a fiction: it has a valuable role in codifying norms of conduct among states that accept those norms. But those states have self-interested motives in interpreting them (hence the many years of UN indulgence of Saddam's serial violation of Security Council resolutions, when certain states had clear commercial reasons for favouring inaction), while malevolent tyrannies do not accept them. It is futile to bemoan the Western democracies' 'readiness to use force in international relations' when implementation of the civilised norms of international law requires the willingness of those same states to use force against aggressors – and, more particularly, against states that harbour and support terrorists who seek the destruction of Western civilisation. Whether, and how, to threaten or exercise that force inevitably requires political judgement. This is inadvertently demonstrated by Sands when he descends from his Olympian perch and ventures a comment on contemporary politics that turns out to be drearily familiar:

> During the Clinton administration a powerful group of neo-conservatives plotted to remake the international order. Their plan was set out in various manifestos, such as the Statement of Principles and other documents associated with the Project for the New American Century.[29]

If the Professor of Law and Director of the Centre on International Courts and Tribunals at University College London believes this is an adequate description of the way US foreign policy is made, and in particular explains the shifts in

US strategic doctrine under President Bush, then, politically speaking, he will believe anything.

The notion of collective security in the 1930s required an ultimate guarantor of peace in a world lacking a sovereign international legal authority, and so does the international order now. That is the threat of superior force wielded by governments whose own legitimacy resides in their democratic character and accountability to accepted norms of conduct. Democracies themselves can, of course, behave in illiberal ways, but so do activist groups that seek to supplant democratic politics by judicial fiat.

## THE IMPORTANCE OF LEGAL PRECEPTS

Yet if liberal-democratic internationalism needs a realism about the progressive character of a rules-based approach to the international order, there can be no dispute among progressives that a sovereign democratic state, acting alone or in concert with allies, must have a regard for due process and its own legal precepts. The most grievous failing of the Bush Administration in its foreign policy has been an indifference to those preconditions of legitimacy.

The anti-totalitarian struggle is one that will probably last decades. What are initially designed in wartime as emergency measures may, therefore, last indefinitely. The inevitable abridgements of liberty that a military campaign requires are not sufficiently well designed to allow us to maintain for long the appearance – and reality – of fairness and due process. Non-governmental organisations such as Human Rights Watch and Amnesty International overreached themselves in the Iraq controversy by (in the first case) presuming competence to judge the justification for war, and (in the second) *complaining* that the British government was publicising Saddam's human rights abuses. But they – and more particularly the Red Cross, whose warnings about Abu Ghraib were not treated with the weight they merited – have an important role to play in shaping policy in this respect. It is essential in the short term that the US administration order a formal system of inspections of detention centres, in which the NGOs should be involved, establish a code of rights for prisoners, and provide for judicial review in cases of terrorist suspects.

In the longer term, progressives must accept that the counterinsurgency war in Iraq is vital to our security and the Iraqis' liberty; and that the security measures we take at home are a price we have to pay for our own protection. But progressives also have a responsibility to warn when we are losing that war – not because the terrorist insurgents are inflicting massive damage on our forces, but because in important respects we have failed the people whose liberation we are responsible for. We cannot make that up by withdrawing from our responsibilities in Iraq and elsewhere. The tortures and deaths in US custody require expiation, not just symbolically but practically, to the people of Iraq, in the form of due process and the rule of law. Those values, so traduced by American gaolers at Abu Ghraib, are exemplified in the arraignment before an Iraqi court of a despot whose regime was founded on torture and killing.

## IS IT NEOCONSERVATISM?

Tony Blair's interventionism is not 'right-wing': it is the reassertion of an earlier left-wing tradition of anti-totalitarianism. Blair's approach has its own flaws, in that it lacks an inherent sense of priorities (for example, promoting democracy in Syria, which genuinely is part of an axis of Islamist terror, is a more urgent task than doing the same in North Korea). But it is immeasurably less flawed than the approach advanced in the 1990s by the Conservative Government of John Major in its policy towards Serb aggression against Bosnia's multi-ethnic democracy. The Major Government adopted not a Burkean scepticism but a Machiavellian cynicism about the limits of effective intervention; among other weaknesses, that realist-Conservative approach has an impossibly narrow view of the national interest. This is particularly dangerous when the totalitarian enemies we now face pursue unlimited ends. Blair, conversely, has an expansive view of the responsibility of the Western democracies in the pursuit of political change, and is properly thought of as the most radical voice on foreign policy in mainstream British politics. With that in mind, I should make a modest plea for claiming the term 'neoconservative' as an accurate designation of a progressive political stance, and of Blair's foreign policies in particular.

Sometime in the first Administration of President Bush his critics discovered (and as we have seen, disseminated into the lexicon of transatlantic political debate) the nefarious designs of a small Washington-based pressure group called the Project for the New American Century (PNAC), which purportedly plotted an aggressive tilt in US foreign policy. The Project's statement of principles on national security issues was a particular cause for concern, as it maintained:

> We seem to have forgotten the essential elements of the Reagan Administration's success: a military that is strong and ready to meet both present and future challenges; a foreign policy that boldly and purposefully promotes American principles abroad; and national leadership that accepts the United States' global responsibilities.

> Of course, the United States must be prudent in how it exercises its power. But we cannot safely avoid the responsibilities of global leadership or the costs that are associated with its exercise. America has a vital role in maintaining peace and security in Europe, Asia, and the Middle East. If we shirk our responsibilities, we invite challenges to our fundamental interests. The history of the 20th century should have taught us that it is important to shape circumstances before crises emerge, and to meet threats before they become dire. The history of this century should have taught us to embrace the cause of American leadership.

Because this was written long before 9/11 – some four years previously, when President Bush was just Governor of Texas – it was taken by Bush's critics to be a long-held covert plan (covert, but available on the Internet[30]) for global domination.

It is, in fact, a fairly unexceptional statement of principles that would accord with what I have argued are progressive

axioms informed by history. The PNAC's declaration over-
states the consistency of the Reagan Administration's approach
to foreign policy – which, as we have seen, encompassed a distinct reversal of approach towards the Soviet Union after
1983; a fundamental difference between Reagan, who believed
in worldwide nuclear disarmament, and his Administration,
who prudently did not; and caution about projecting American
power, certainly as compared with the policies of all his suc-
cessors to date. But it is otherwise, with one exception, a
straightforward assertion of traditional liberal-democratic
internationalism. The exception is the absence of a reference
to the role of international institutions. It is more Reaganite
(liberal-nationalist) than Wilsonian (liberal-internationalist).

There does seem to be a need for a descriptive term for the
promotion of global democracy on both idealistic and pragmatic grounds, coupled with a scepticism about a 'top-down'
approach of disseminating civilised values by applying universal rules. Neoconservatism is far from ideal, but it will do if
certain caveats are borne in mind.

It is one of the myths of modern politics that neoconservatism is a movement of the Right. The term neconservatism
was coined as a derogatory label by the Socialist leader
Michael Harrington in 1976 to refer to those on the Left who
were active in the cause of strengthening America's defences in
the Cold War. These were generally Democrats and supporters
of Senator Henry 'Scoop' Jackson, who had unsuccessfully
sought the Democratic presidential nomination in 1972 and
1976. Many of them later served in the Reagan Administration (such as Richard Perle, an aide to Jackson, and Jeane
Kirkpatrick). The term was popularised in a hostile book by
Peter Steinfels in 1979.[31]

One of the problems of Steinfels's argument was that it
applied the term 'neoconservative' almost indiscriminately –
for example, to the liberal Democrat Daniel Patrick Moynihan.
So far as I am aware, only one designated American neoconservative – Irving Kristol – has ever voluntarily adopted a label
that (like 'Methodist' in an earlier generation) was originally
intended to be dismissive. Applying it both to Kristol and to

such figures as his social democratic friends Daniel Bell (a sociologist) and the late Sidney Hook (a philosopher) obscures more than it elucidates, but it is a term that nonetheless has gained popularity among political correspondents of (or rather, below) a certain age. An attempt by the *New Statesman* in 2003 to identify a cabal (which seems to be the favoured collective term) of half a dozen neoconservatives in the British press foundered on the fact that only one of them (political columnist Stephen Pollard) had ever owned up to being one. The others included social democrats and traditional conservatives with no obvious common characteristic apart from support for the Iraq War.[32]

More sensibly and at the same time, the liberal American *New Republic* commented on the difficulty of distinguishing neoconservatism from neoliberalism in current foreign policy debates:

> [A]s a practical matter, what's the difference between these two positions? Few neocons would insist that preemption should be the option you turn to first. Meanwhile, most honest observers would concede that if Iraq falls into the category of countries for which preemption is justified as a last resort, then there are probably four or five other countries for which preemption could be similarly justified. In any case, all of that is beside the point, since even the most hawkish neocons rarely advocate preemptively attacking any one of those remaining candidates.[33]

But the caveat is that support for an assertive foreign policy, an uncompromising war on Islamist terror, and a mix of economic, diplomatic and (where necessary, as in Baathist Iraq) military pressure to bring down totalitarian states of both secular and theocratic varieties is not necessarily a characteristic of those usually termed neoconservatives! Irving Kristol is sceptical of the case for spreading democracy overseas. Another influential neoconservative, Norman Podhoretz, has claimed there is no longer a difference between neoconservatism and plain conservatism, while his magazine, *Commentary*, is a forum for reactionary social views on such issues as gay rights and, astonishingly for the 21st century, Darwinism.

If neoconservatives such as Podhoretz are abandoning the term, this is as good a time as any to adopt it. No longer would neoconservatism necessarily denote rage at the cultural changes of the 1960s. It would encompass those of us who believe the cultural changes of the 1960s have had a civilising effect and ought to go further.

Neoconservatism emerged from the Henry Jackson wing of liberalism, which stressed the importance in foreign policy of the promotion of democracy and human rights. It was one strand of the politics of the Reagan Administration, but only one. It was perhaps best exemplified by Paul Wolfowitz, who influenced the Administration to oppose President Ferdinand Marcos's electoral fraud in the Philippines in 1986 and support pressure for democracy in South Korea in 1987. It also encapsulates the philosophy of one of the lesser-known but most important legacies of the Reagan years: the National Endowment for Democracy (NED), established in 1984 by the US government as a private institute to award grants to American organisations that work directly with foreign counterparts to foster democratic institutions (e.g. trade unions). The NED supported Solidarity in Poland and the Command for the No in Chile under Pinochet.

These practical aspects of neoconservatism are progressive and humanitarian, and characteristic of the principles of liberal-democratic internationalism. They are, moreover, not the preserve of any one political party. At times, historically and also recently (in Bosnia and Kosovo, and, in the case of the British Tories, in Iraq now), the Republicans and the British Conservative Party have been the apostles of isolationism and believers in narrow constraints on the exercise of national power. The Left (including now the British Liberal Democrats) has notoriously been infected with a reactionary preference for stability rather than liberty in the international order. Progressive politics require that these elements be challenged wherever they appear.

## A PROGRESSIVE COALITION

Interventionism has proved a political liability for Tony Blair. It is essential that it receive the support of progressive internationalists, but it is also important that regime change be a bipartisan cause. Despite the cynicism of today's Conservative Party and the Liberal Democrats, there are grounds for a synthesis of view among people of differing political philosophies. The distinction between realism and idealism is no longer relevant when there is a direct connection between the overthrow of tyranny and the defence of national security.

The Left has a historic responsibility in this task, to be true to its legacy whatever the position of parties of the Right. It should recognise that its finest ideals are now enshrined in US policy, and commit itself to global democracy. If it fails to do so, it will betray the cause of internationalism and anti-totalitarianism, and will risk the resurgence of a conservative *realpolitik* in informal alliance with an isolationist and reactionary Left.

1 Tony Benn, *Free at Last: Diaries 1991–2001* (London: Random House, 2002), p. 273.
2 Peter Jones, *America and the British Labour Party* (London: Tauris Academic Studies, 1997), pp. 230–1.
3 John Kampfner, *Blair's Wars* (London: Free Press, 2004).
4 Paul Berman, *Terror and Liberalism* (New York: W. W. Norton, 2003), p. 210.
5 Matthew Parris, 'Why I will be rooting for a George Bush election victory', *The Times*, 8 May 2004.
6 Fareed Zakaria, *The Future of Freedom: Illiberal Democracy at Home and Abroad* (New York: W. W. Norton, 2003).
7 On this problem, see a stimulating short book by a young American lawyer, Noah Feldman, on the ethics and aims of nation-building, *What We Owe Iraq* (Princeton: Princeton University Press, 2004). Feldman writes from the vantage point of having served as Senior Constitutional Adviser to the Coalition Provisional Authority in Iraq. He argues for a humble rather than expansive approach to nation-building, concentrating on providing security, and maintains that we have an obligation to remain in Iraq until its government has a monopoly of force.

8 Stephen Holmes, 'Must democracy wait?', *American Prospect*, Vol. 14, Issue 6, 2003.

9 Brian Brivati, 'Sneering will not help democracy', *Guardian*, 26 February 2005.

10 Data from UNICEF, at
http://www.unicef.org/infobycountry/mali_statistics.html

11 According to a senior British diplomat involved in the negotiations, Michael Alexander, in his posthumous memoir *Managing the Cold War* (London: RUSI, 2005, p. 62): 'These texts [the Helsinki Final Agreement] provided a crucial and perhaps decisive encouragement to the dissident movements in Eastern Europe. Leading Soviet dissidents, including the Sakharovs, Yuri Orlov and Anatoly Scharansky based their Helsinki monitoring activities on their duty to play their part in ensuring that the Soviet government complied with the obligations it had undertaken at Helsinki.'

12 Speech available at
http://www.number-10.gov.uk/output/Page4220.asp

13 Noam Chomsky, *The Prosperous Few and the Restless Many* (London: Pluto Press, 1994); available at
http://www.zmag.org/chomsky/pfrm/pfrm-05.html

14 The episode is recounted by Brendan Simms, *Unfinest Hour: Britain and the Destruction of Bosnia* (London: Allen Lane, 2001), p. 96. I also owe to Simms the term 'conservative pessimism' as a description of the Major Government's approach.

15 Cited in Dave Rich, 'The barriers come down – antisemitism and coalitions of extremes', Institute for Jewish Policy Research, 2004, at
http://www.axt.org.uk/HateMusic/rich_essay_nov_04.pdf

16 'Many thinkers and historians have exposed the lies of the Zionists, thus becoming a target of Zionist persecution. Some have been assassinated, some arrested, and some are prevented from making a living. For example, Jewish associations and organizations have filed lawsuits against famous French philosopher Roger Garaudy, who in 1995 published his book *The Founding Myths of Israeli Politics* in which he disproves the myth of the "gas chambers," saying, "This idea is not technically possible. So far, no one has clarified how these false gas chambers worked, and what proof there is of their existence. Anyone with proof of their existence must show it." British historian David Irving was also sued, while Austrian author Gerd Honsik was sentenced to 18 months' imprisonment because he wrote a number of articles denying the existence of the gas chambers in the Nazi detention camps.' This farrago of nonsense was published by

Rantissi in a Hamas weekly, and has been translated by the Middle East Media Research Institute at http://memri.org/bin/articles.cgi?Page=archives&Area=sd&ID=SP55803

17 Nick Cohen, 'The lesson the Left has never learnt', *New Statesman*, 21 July 2003.

18 Andrew Murray and Lindsey German, respectively Chairman and Convenor of the Stop the War Coalition, say on p. 86 of their book *Stop the War: The Story of Britain's Biggest Mass Movement* (London: Bookmarks, 2005), 'MAB's actual objectives are clear and reasonable'. Murray is a leading member of the Communist Party of Britain and advocate of 'solidarity with People's [i.e. North] Korea' (see his 'political report' to the Party's executive committee, March 2003, at http://www.communist-party.org.uk/articles/2003/march/10-03-03.shtml). German until recently edited the monthly journal of the Socialist Workers' Party, whose immediate response to 9/11 was 'We do not believe that the use of the word "condemn" is appropriate in relation to the tragic events in the US' (statement presented to the executive of the Socialist Alliance, and available at http://www.cpgb.org.uk/worker/400/response.html#swpresponse). What is reasonable to them may not accord with the conventional use of the term.

19 On this movement, see Richard Griffiths, *Fascism* (London: Continuum, 2005), Chapter 8, on which this paragraph draws, and Zeev Sternhell, *Neither Right nor Left: Fascist Ideology in France* (Princeton: Princeton University Press, 1986), Chapters 4 and 5.

20 'The best response to war would be protests across the globe which make it impossible for Bush and Blair to continue. But while war lasts by far the lesser evil would be reverses, or defeat, for the US and British forces.' See the *Socialist Worker*, 23 March 2003.

21 In an open letter published on the party's web site, SWP ideologue Alex Callinicos of York University clearly indicated that he believed 'road-side bombs that kill American soldiers and attacks on Iraqi recruits to the puppet regime's army and police and on its officials' were 'legitimate attacks'. For the full text of the letter see http://www.zmag.org/content/showarticle.cfm?SectionID=15&ItemID=7016 For an example of an attack on 'the puppet regime's' functionaries, see http://news.bbc.co.uk/1/hi/world/middle_east/4303629.stm

22 Nicholas Goodrick-Clarke gives a fascinating account of the bizarre notions of Evola and his later followers, including Griffin, in *Black Sun: Aryan Cults, Esoteric Nazism and the Politics of Identity* (New York: New York University Press, 2002), pp. 52–71.

23 Philippe Sands, *Lawless World – America and the Making and Breaking of Global Rules* (London: Allen Lane, 2005), p. xviii.

24 It is worth noting that other international lawyers maintain that adequate authorisation for war was provided by UN Security Council Resolutions 678 and 687, which established the terms of the ceasefire in the first Gulf War and which Saddam then violated. I am grateful to Professor Colleen Graffy for advice on this point. See also Christopher Greenwood (Professor of International Law at the LSE, who assisted the Government in the Iraq War), 'Britain's war on Saddam had the law on its side', *The Times*, 22 October 2003.

25 'Barrister of the bloody heart', interview in *The Age*, 11 June 2005.

26 For an account of the case see the WTO's web site at http://www.wto.org/english/thewto_e/whatis_e/tif_e/disp3_e.htm

27 I owe this distinction to Francis Fukuyama, *State-Building* (London: Profile Books, 2004), pp. 149–50. A recent erudite exposition of the Lockean theory of liberal constitutionalism is Jeremy Rabkin, *Law Without Nations? Why Constitutional Government Requires Sovereign States* (Princeton: Princeton University Press, 2004).

28 Greenpeace International, '"Preventive war" and international law after Iraq', 22 May 2003; available at http://www.greenpeace.org/raw/content/international/press/reports/preventive-war-and-internati.pdf

29 Sands, *Lawless World*, p. 20.

30 Here: http://www.newamericancentury.org/statementofprinciples.htm

31 Peter Steinfels, *The Neoconservatives: The Men who are Changing America's Politics* (New York: Simon and Schuster, 1979).

32 The others were John Lloyd and David Aaronovitch, both from the social-democratic Left; Daniel Finkelstein and Michael Gove, both Conservatives; and Melanie Phillips, an idiosyncratic communitarian.

33 '&c., A Daily Journal of Politics', *New Republic Online*, 22 July 2003.

# THE AUTHOR

Oliver Kamm is a columnist for *The Times*, a political and cultural commentator on television and radio, and one of the founders of a new financial services group, WMG Advisors LLP. He was born in 1963 in London, and studied at the universities of Oxford and London. He began his career in the International Division of the Bank of England, and has been European Equity Strategist for HSBC Securities, and Head of Strategic Research and Adviser on Business Strategy at Commerzbank Securities.

He is a former Chairman of the Oxford University Labour Club. From 1997 to 2001 he was adviser to the Independent MP Martin Bell. He is a member of Chatham House and a patron of the Henry Jackson Society, named for the late US Senator who advanced the cause of liberal anti-totalitarianism in Congress from 1952 to 1983. His web log is at http://oliverkamm.typepad.com